OPPOSING
VIEWPOINTS®
SERIES

# Privilege in America

# Other Books of Related Interest

## Opposing Viewpoints Series

Black Lives Matter
Gentrification and the Housing Crisis
Identity Politics
Race in America
The Wealth Gap

## At Issue Series

Environmental Racism and Classism
Gender Politics
Male Privilege
Student Debt
Universal Health Care

## Current Controversies Series

Are There Two Americas?
Homelessness and Street Crime
Learned Helplessness, Welfare, and the Poverty Cycle
LGBTQ Rights
The Political Elite and Special Interests

# "Congress shall make no law ... abridging the freedom of speech, or of the press."

*First Amendment to the US Constitution*

The basic foundation of our democracy is the First Amendment guarantee of freedom of expression. The Opposing Viewpoints series is dedicated to the concept of this basic freedom and the idea that it is more important to practice it than to enshrine it.

OPPOSING
VIEWPOINTS®
SERIES

# | Privilege in America

Gary Wiener, Book Editor

GREENHAVEN
PUBLISHING

Published in 2020 by Greenhaven Publishing, LLC
353 3rd Avenue, Suite 255, New York, NY 10010

Articles in Greenhaven Publishing anthologies are often edited for length to meet page
requirements. In addition, original titles of these works are changed to clearly present
the main thesis and to explicitly indicate the author's opinion. Every effort is made to
ensure that Greenhaven Publishing accurately reflects the original intent of the authors.
Every effort has been made to trace the owners of the copyrighted material.

Cover image: Sean Locke Photography/Shutterstock.com

**Library of Congress Cataloging-in-Publication Data**

Names: Wiener, Gary, editor.
Title: Privilege in America / Gary Wiener, book editor.
Description: First edition. | New York : Greenhaven Publishing, 2020. | Series: Opposing
viewpoints | Includes bibliographical references and index. | Audience: Grades 9–12.
Identifiers: LCCN 2019022599 | ISBN 9781534506039 (library
binding) | ISBN 9781534506022 (paperback)
Subjects: LCSH: Privilege (Social psychology)—Juvenile literature. | Equality—
Juvenile literature. | Power (Social sciences)—Juvenile literature.
Classification: LCC HM671 .P752 2020 | DDC 303.3—dc23
LC record available at https://lccn.loc.gov/2019022599

*Manufactured in the United States of America*

Website: http://greenhavenpublishing.com

# Contents

## Chapter 3: How Does Male Privilege Affect Women?

## Chapter 4: What Steps Can Be Taken to Even the Playing Field?

# The Importance of Opposing Viewpoints

Perhaps every generation experiences a period in time in which the populace seems especially polarized, starkly divided on the important issues of the day and gravitating toward the far ends of the political spectrum and away from a consensus-facilitating middle ground. The world that today's students are growing up in and that they will soon enter into as active and engaged citizens is deeply fragmented in just this way. Issues relating to terrorism, immigration, women's rights, minority rights, race relations, health care, taxation, wealth and poverty, the environment, policing, military intervention, the proper role of government—in some ways, perennial issues that are freshly and uniquely urgent and vital with each new generation—are currently roiling the world.

If we are to foster a knowledgeable, responsible, active, and engaged citizenry among today's youth, we must provide them with the intellectual, interpretive, and critical-thinking tools and experience necessary to make sense of the world around them and of the all-important debates and arguments that inform it. After all, the outcome of these debates will in large measure determine the future course, prospects, and outcomes of the world and its peoples, particularly its youth. If they are to become successful members of society and productive and informed citizens, students need to learn how to evaluate the strengths and weaknesses of someone else's arguments, how to sift fact from opinion and fallacy, and how to test the relative merits and validity of their own opinions against the known facts and the best possible available information. The landmark series Opposing Viewpoints has been providing students with just such critical-thinking skills and exposure to the debates surrounding society's most urgent contemporary issues for many years, and it continues to serve this essential role with undiminished commitment, care, and rigor.

The key to the series's success in achieving its goal of sharpening students' critical-thinking and analytic skills resides in its title—

Opposing Viewpoints. In every intriguing, compelling, and engaging volume of this series, readers are presented with the widest possible spectrum of distinct viewpoints, expert opinions, and informed argumentation and commentary, supplied by some of today's leading academics, thinkers, analysts, politicians, policy makers, economists, activists, change agents, and advocates. Every opinion and argument anthologized here is presented objectively and accorded respect. There is no editorializing in any introductory text or in the arrangement and order of the pieces. No piece is included as a "straw man," an easy ideological target for cheap point-scoring. As wide and inclusive a range of viewpoints as possible is offered, with no privileging of one particular political ideology or cultural perspective over another. It is left to each individual reader to evaluate the relative merits of each argument— as he or she sees it, and with the use of ever-growing critical-thinking skills—and grapple with his or her own assumptions, beliefs, and perspectives to determine how convincing or successful any given argument is and how the reader's own stance on the issue may be modified or altered in response to it.

This process is facilitated and supported by volume, chapter, and selection introductions that provide readers with the essential context they need to begin engaging with the spotlighted issues, with the debates surrounding them, and with their own perhaps shifting or nascent opinions on them. In addition, guided reading and discussion questions encourage readers to determine the authors' point of view and purpose, interrogate and analyze the various arguments and their rhetoric and structure, evaluate the arguments' strengths and weaknesses, test their claims against available facts and evidence, judge the validity of the reasoning, and bring into clearer, sharper focus the reader's own beliefs and conclusions and how they may differ from or align with those in the collection or those of their classmates.

Research has shown that reading comprehension skills improve dramatically when students are provided with compelling, intriguing, and relevant "discussable" texts. The subject matter of these collections could not be more compelling, intriguing, or urgently relevant to today's students and the world they are poised to inherit. The anthologized articles and the reading and discussion questions that are included with them also provide the basis for stimulating, lively, and passionate classroom debates. Students who are compelled to anticipate objections to their own argument and identify the flaws in those of an opponent read more carefully, think more critically, and steep themselves in relevant context, facts, and information more thoroughly. In short, using discussable text of the kind provided by every single volume in the Opposing Viewpoints series encourages close reading, facilitates reading comprehension, fosters research, strengthens critical thinking, and greatly enlivens and energizes classroom discussion and participation. The entire learning process is deepened, extended, and strengthened.

For all of these reasons, Opposing Viewpoints continues to be exactly the right resource at exactly the right time—when we most need to provide readers with the critical-thinking tools and skills that will not only serve them well in school but also in their careers and their daily lives as decision-making family members, community members, and citizens. This series encourages respectful engagement with and analysis of opposing viewpoints and fosters a resulting increase in the strength and rigor of one's own opinions and stances. As such, it helps make readers "future ready," and that readiness will pay rich dividends for the readers themselves, for the citizenry, for our society, and for the world at large.

# Introduction

> *"Being part of a 'privileged' group does not mean you are guilty of atrocities against a less privileged group such as these. We need to de-stigmatize both 'bias' and 'privilege.' Setting aside the judgment and defensiveness that arise from these terms, we can look honestly at them—and overcome their negative consequences."*[1]

"Privilege" is a word that is thrown around a lot in today's discourse. Some would say it's overused. But what do we mean when we talk about privilege? A stark example of the concept can be seen by contrasting the last two US presidents, one black, one white. The black man, Barack Obama, is ostensibly a good family man: never divorced, no known affairs, two children with his wife. The second, Donald J. Trump, is lauded by his followers—even Evangelical Christians—as a good family man. Yet he has had three wives, has cheated on all three (including his now very public dalliance with an adult film star), and his five children are a product of those three different wives. What's striking about this comparison?

Turn the profiles around. Would Barack Obama have been elected president if he'd had Donald Trump's history? Only the most naïve political observers would answer this question affirmatively.

Yet privilege is rarely simple or clear cut. Often, as many observers have noted, it is invisible to those who have it. As Peggy McIntosh famously wrote, "I have come to see white privilege as an invisible package of unearned assets that I can count on cashing in each day, but about which I was 'meant' to remain oblivious. White privilege is like an invisible weightless knapsack of special provisions, maps, passports, codebooks, visas, clothes, tools and blank checks."[2]

Scholars date the emergence of what is now called "privilege theory" to the writings of African-American scholar W.E.B. Du Bois. In his classic treatise, *The Souls of Black Folks (1903)*, Du Bois wrote that although African Americans were highly aware of white Americans and racial discrimination, Whites did not think much about African-Americans, nor about the consequences of discrimination. In the 1930s, Du Bois wrote of the "wages of whiteness," whereby Southern white workers might feel superior to their black peers:

> … the white group of laborers, while they receive a low wage, were compensated in part by a sort of public and psychological wage. They were given public deference and titles of courtesy because they were white. They were admitted freely with all classes of white people to public functions, public parks, and the best schools.[3]

But discussions around privilege really took off with the work of Peggy McIntosh, and the publication of her essay "White Privilege and Male Privilege: A Personal Account of Coming to See Correspondences through Work in Women's Studies." Here McIntosh documents a range of privileges she and others like her enjoyed simply by virtue of having white skin. McIntosh's seminal essay has sparked the ever-expanding study of privilege in America, and, moreover, the rest of the world.

We now understand that there are many more types of privilege than white privilege. Feminists and their supporters speak of male privilege as that invisible barrier that keeps them from joining "the boy's club" in business and society. LBGTQ individuals and their supporters study heterosexual privilege. Those in minority religions have seen the effects of Christian privilege in the United States, noting how Christians who commit mass murders are referred to as merely deranged or insane, but Muslims who do the same are branded as dangerous terrorists, religious extremists who want to alter the fabric of society. Another common form of privilege is socio-economic: the parents who bribed their children's way into the University of Southern California (USC) and Yale University had a form of privilege that only money could buy.

With so many forms of privilege now identified, it would seem that everyone walking the streets of the United States benefits from some type of privilege, as Peggy McIntosh realized when, in considering male privileges, she came to understand that she was the beneficiary of similar advantages as a white person. The notion that everyone except perhaps the most abject members of society has some form of privilege is arguably valid. African-American writer Damon Young has written a piece entitled "Straight Black Males are the White People of Black People" in which he observed that "Intraracially … our relationship to and with black women is not unlike whiteness's relationship to us. In fact, it's eerily similar."[4] In an essay entitled "Black Americans, It's Time We Recognize Our Privilege … Our American Privilege" Arah Iloabugichukwu lists more than two dozen specific ways in which having the "blue [American] passport" brings with it powerful entitlements. "My fellow Americans, the game has been rigged in our favor," she writes.[5]

With the advent of privilege theory and its entrance into popular culture, the potential for inappropriate use of its ideas is always present. For example, there is "privilege check," where a marginalized member of society accuses a more privileged person of being insensitive. This usually takes the form of the less privileged person ordering the other to "check your privilege." Such admonitions have often led the more privileged party to bristle and have usually increased friction rather than leading to open and fruitful discourse. As Peggy McIntosh has suggested, in practical terms the privilege check functions as the closest thing we have to a racial slur directed at straight white males.

Then, too, there is what has been derisively called the "Privilege Olympics," where one under-privileged member of society tries to assert that he or she is less privileged than others because they benefit from fewer privileges. Such "contests" are not really beneficial to furthering societal discourse because they devolve into a match to determine who is more worthy of support. But as *Washington Post* columnist Esther Cepeda writes, "Does it really matter whether we think we have—or lack—some privilege relative to others? Does it move us forward in any meaningful way?" As Cepeda concludes, "Perhaps it's time to stop focusing on how our particular privileges help us and start thinking about how to use whatever privileges we may possess to make others' lives better—regardless of whether we agree with their politics."[6]

Indeed, the entire point of the privilege question should focus on how society can improve everyone's lot in life, and not how individuals can bemoan their lowly status. In chapters titled "Is Privilege a Serious Problem in America?" "What Does White Privilege Mean?" "How Does Male Privilege Affect Women?" and "What Steps Can Be Taken to Even the Playing Field?" *Opposing Viewpoints: Privilege in America* presents a wide range of viewpoints concerning whether privilege exists, whether it is actually a serious problem in society, how privilege affects marginalized populations, and how best to deal with the problem in practical terms.

## Notes

1. "What Is Privilege? Is It a Four-Letter Word?" by Caroline Turner, HuffPost, September 27, 2016.
2. Peggy McIntosh, "White Privilege: Unpacking the Invisible Knapsack," *Peace and Freedom Magazine*, July/August, 1989, pp. 10-12.
3. Quoted in Adolph Reed, Jr., Du Bois and the "Wages of Whiteness." NonSite.org. June 29, 2017. https://nonsite.org/editorial/du-bois-and-the-wages-of-whiteness
4. Damon Young, "Straight Black Males are the White People of Black People." VSB. Sept. 9, 2017. https://verysmartbrothas.theroot.com/straight-black-men-are-the-white-people-of-black-people-1814157214
5. Arah Iloabugichukwu, "Black Americans, It's Time We Recognize Our Privilege… Our American Privilege." MadameNoir. March 28, 2018. https://madamenoire.com/1019443/reader-submission-black-americans-its-time-we-recognize-our-privilege-our-american-privilege/
6. Esther J. Cepeda, "No One Wins the oppression Olympics." The Chicago Tribune. Oct. 11, 2017. https://www.chicagotribune.com/suburbs/post-tribune/opinion/ct-ptb-cepeda-oppression-st-1012-20171011-story.html

# Is Privilege a Serious Problem in America?

# Chapter Preface

Much has been written about privilege and its various manifestations. Those on the political left see it as an ingrained societal issue that affects all marginalized people. Those on the right scoff at it and grow indignant when they are accused of reaping privilege's benefits. To many who carry their invisible knapsacks of privileges on their back, privilege is not a problem because they do not understand how others live. They are used to reaping the benefits of privilege and do not see what the problem is.

Because privilege has become such a prominent social issue in the twenty-first century, there has been an expected backlash from those who object to being told "Check your privilege."

Essays that denounce the concept of privilege are regularly met with a barrage of progressive attacks, but they nevertheless make their point and occasion spirited debate. In May of 2014, Princeton college freshman Tal Fortgang published an essay in *Time* magazine entitled "Why I'll Never Apologize for my White Male Privilege." In it, Fortgang, who had been instructed to check his privilege on more than one occasion, wrote about how his ancestors survived the Holocaust, came to America "with no money and no English," and worked extraordinarily hard for everything they earned in life. The problem with calling people out as privileged, he argues, "You don't know what their struggles have been, what they may have gone through to be where they are. Assuming they've benefitted from 'power systems or other conspiratorial imaginary institutions denies them credit for all they've done, things of which you may not even conceive."

Near his conclusion, Fortgang writes, "Behind every success, large or small, there is a story, and it isn't always told by sex or skin color." Within days of the publication of his essay, Fortgang was rebutted by a fellow Princetonian, Briana Payton, also in *Time* magazine. Her equally strongly worded essay was entitled "Dear Privileged-at-Princeton: You. Are. Privileged. And Meritocracy Is a Myth." In it, she wrote that Fortgang clearly did not understand the meaning of privilege: "Privilege is not an idea aimed at muting opinion or understating the worth of accomplishments. It is not a stab at personal character, nor is it something for which one needs to apologize." Payton was correct in her assertion that Fortgang had misrepresented the nature of privilege. Ironically, however, the tone and tenor of her essay suggests a stab at Fortgang's personal character, and that he should apologize for his misguided beliefs.

Such is often the nature of privilege debates.

One might imagine that you could put these two Ivy Leaguers in a room to hash out their differences and that they would never come to agreement. The two sides seem that far apart.

> *"Instructions to check our privilege assert that we cannot insist people of different backgrounds and experiences should share our precise political concerns, and that issues which concern members of a vulnerable group cannot be discounted as trivial."*

# "Check Your Privilege" Is Simply a Call for Time Out

*Ally Fogg*

*In the following viewpoint Ally Fogg writes of the complexities of the debate over privilege, and of so-called "identity politics," from a straight, white male perspective. The author observes that while he is in favor of the general idea of checking one's privilege and understanding how a person may receive favored societal status, just because one is reminded of one's privilege does not mean that he is necessarily in the wrong. The call to check one's privilege opens an avenue for self reflection, but it should not be used as a weapon. Ally Fogg is a writer and journalist based in Manchester, England, and a cofounder of the Men & Boys Coalition.*

"'Check Your Privilege' Isn't a Trump Card—It's a Call for Time Out," by Ally Fogg, Guardian News and Media Limited, January 23, 2013. Reprinted by permission.

As you read, consider the following questions:

1. What is intersectionalism, and how does it come into play with regard to privilege?
2. How should a privileged member of society respond to privilege checks, according to Fogg?
3. What bothers Fogg more than privilege checking?

L ike all men of a certain age, I am regularly implored to check my stools for signs of bowel disease, my testicles for unusual lumps and my opinions for symptoms of privilege. All three tasks are distasteful, undesirable and best conducted privately in a moment of quiet contemplation. All three are probably worth the effort.

You may have noticed a bit of a gender-related stooshie in media circles recently. I have no wish to reopen that wound, but a related debate that has been running for a while was brought into sharp focus by recent events. There is palpable resentment among sections of the commentariat that their readers and online correspondents sometimes like to remind them of their privilege. It is significant that such complaints usually come from the centre left, not the right. People who would never criticise feminism or anti-racism projects suddenly start grumbling about identity politics when asked to consider not just a single axis of oppression (patriarchy or racism) but several simultaneously. It is surely not coincidental that their problems with identity politics seem to arise at the precise moment they are reminded of their own multiple privileges, or if you prefer, when identity politics moves from the sectional to the intersectional.

Identity politics can easily become a kind of oppression Olympics, with the winner the one wearing the most section badges of oppression. Intersectional analysis does not add to that puzzle so much as attempt to solve it. It implies that you cannot address forms of oppression in isolation, that you cannot argue that injustices facing some parts of society are a distraction from bigger issues, and that you should be aware that your words and deeds can serve to exclude potential allies from that fight or even add to their oppression.

In social theory, according to Peggy McIntosh's classic metaphor, privilege is: "an invisible, weightless backpack of special provisions, maps, passports, codebooks, visas, clothes, tools and blank checks". It is not the same as power, wealth or control, and is no guarantee of such rewards, it is better thought of as a mechanism which societies use to ensure power, wealth and control remain concentrated in the usual hands. The most important aspect to privilege is that we are often unaware of it. Since the lives of the privileged are described as, portrayed as and experienced as the norm, other experiences are seen as aberrant deviations from how things should be. For example, leaving aside the validity of the sums and arguments about the gender pay gap, it is striking that it is almost invariably presented as the average women earning 20% (or whatever) less than the average man, not as the average man being 20% overpaid. The male experience is considered par, standardised at 100%.

Alternatively, I am not oblivious to the irony that when the stalwarts of Cif's You Tell Us wanted an objective and fair-minded overview of concepts of privilege, they requested a straight, white, middle class man for the gig. Consider it an exercise in self-referential satire.

There are many philosophical and political problems with privilege theory. The complex mechanics of oppression are not simple or self-evident and academics can and do devote lifetimes to debating the detail. Personally I believe that most of us are oppressed in various ways by economic systems, and that racism, sexism, class prejudice and the rest are actively fostered and sustained by the demands of capital. Socially prescribed gender roles, for example, can be oppressive for men too, which would imply that female privilege must be acknowledged in some contexts.

The obscuring of male victims of domestic and sexual violence would be a case in point, as would the equating of parenthood with motherhood. The counter-argument, that accruing wealth,

# THE IMPACTS OF PRIVILEGE

Privilege unexamined and unchallenged, pits groups against each other, because they are treated differently by society, organizations and institutions. Members of different groups experience the world in different ways...and operate on different realities. Let's say that I have worked in a large corporation for a number of years and gender has never been an issue for me. I do not even consider gender, it has never led to me sticking out, and I have never felt that the way I have been treated and judged by others was being filtered through the lens of gender. I feel that I am treated as an individual, not based on the social groups that I belong to. Gender is a non-issue for me.

And then I hear a co-worker talk about how gender has always been an issue in her professional life. Maybe she says that she has had to work harder and be better than her male peers to be taken seriously, has always had to go the extra mile as she has not had the benefit of membership in the "old boys club."

Based on my experience of gender as a non-issue, it is pretty easy for me to be doubtful. I do not think people are treated according to gender, I think they are treated as individuals...because that has been my experience. I might even be offended by what she says because I have worked hard, nothing has been given to me. I might think she is playing the "gender card," trying to game the system.

Examining and challenging privilege requires empathy. It requires that I have healthy, candid relationships with people of different identities and experiences. I have to have a relationship with my co-worker which includes conversations about her experience in our organization as a woman so that I am able to understand ways in which we are treated differently.

So.

Do you have relationships within your organization with people that have different identities and experiences than you do?

Do you have relationships that are healthy enough to have conversations about different experiences related to race, gender, age, orientation, etc.?

Do you think that the employee experience in your organization is different for people based on things like race, gender, age or orientation?

"The Impacts of Privilege," Joe Gerstandt, March 21, 2012.

power and career progression is everyone's primary ambition while domestic and relationship sacrifices are simply costs of dominance, strikes me as yet another privileged, middle-class perspective. Instructions to check our privilege remind us of these complexities. They assert that we cannot insist people of different backgrounds and experiences should share our precise political concerns, and that issues which concern members of a vulnerable group cannot be discounted as trivial. They do not mean that one perspective is necessarily wrong, just that it cannot be assumed to be correct or the whole story.

As a straight white middle-class male with an interest in gender issues, I am inevitably accused of abuse of privilege and "mansplaining". Sometimes it strikes me as disingenuous, an attempt to close down discussion or restrict the voices in a debate to preferred perspectives. Sometimes it is entirely deserved, and with hindsight I'll agree that yes, I was being a condescending jerk. At other times I will think I've checked my privilege, and I'm sorry but I still don't agree with you. That is not an abuse of privilege, but an essential option in an inclusive debate. A privilege check is not really a trump card in a debate, so much as a call for a time out for tactical reappraisal by those on our own side. That strikes me as no bad thing.

Privilege-checking can be irritating and frustrating, but it bothers me less than pronouncements from those with the highest platforms and largest megaphones demanding acquiescence to their status, acceptance of their values and the right to police the tone or limit the range of objections of their detractors. Now that really is an abuse of privilege.

> *"White men in Australia, North America and Europe are the beneficiaries of the single greatest affirmative action program in the history of the world."*

# Privilege Is a Problem in the Workplace

**Fiona Smith**

*In the following viewpoint Fiona Smith argues that when it comes to discussions about gender, too often people confuse the term with women's issues. This is because privilege is invisible to those who have it. The absence of men in gender discussions is a problem, precisely because men usually have no problems with their gender. Usually, men become involved in gender issues only when they see women and girls whom they love facing discrimination. Men need to be convinced that gender equality is good for everyone, and this notion often starts in the home. Fiona Smith is an Australian journalist whose work is seen in* Bloomberg News, *the* Guardian, *the* Sydney Morning Herald, *the* Miami Herald, *and the* Seattle Times, *among other publications.*

"'Privilege Is Invisible to Those Who Have It': Engaging Men in Workplace Equality," by Fiona Smith, Guardian News and Media Limited, June 8, 2016. Reprinted by permission.

As you read, consider the following questions:

1. According to Smith, how is privilege invisible to those who have it?
2. What are some obstacles to gender equality?
3. How does gender equality make everyone happier?

Turn up to any meeting on gender equality and the room will be full of women. Women talking to women about women.

When it comes to advancing women in the workplace, one of the biggest hurdles is men's lack of interest. According to American sociologist, Prof Michael Kimmel, men can't see what the issue is. They don't see the advantages conferred by their Y chromosome.

"Privilege is invisible to those who have it."

Kimmel, author and distinguished professor of sociology and gender studies at New York's Stony Brook University, was in Sydney recently to talk about how to engage more men in the discussion around gender equality at work.

Privilege comes in a myriad of forms, including race, gender, wealth, physical fitness, safety, and educational attainment and indeed height. However, the people who have those things are usually unaware of their power and influence.

"I am the generic person. I am a middle class white man. I have no race, no class, no gender. I am universally generalisable," says Kimmel.

While white, middle class men may be oblivious to their inherited advantages, those who differ from the norm are always being made aware of their difference, whether it is because of the street harassment endured by young women or the fact that people with foreign-sounding names have to lodge more than 60% more applications to get hired as their Anglo-Celtic rivals.

This obliviousness is often why men don't turn up to workshops on gender equality and why there is such resistance to corrective mechanisms such as gender targets at work. Too many men still believe in the myth of the level playing field and that the word "gender" is another synonym for "women."

A report by KPMG for the ASX corporate governance council released in May demonstrates how many employers are just paying lip service to diversity policies, by implementing them without targets for inclusion.

Kimmel, who has spent his career studying men and masculinity, says the absence of men in gender discussions is a problem.

"We cannot fully empower women and girls without engaging boys and men. We know this to be true. The question is then, how do we get men engaged in this conversation?," asks Kimmel.

## Make Gender Visible

Obliviousness to gender is the first obstacle to recruiting men to the cause of gender equality, he says. "We have to make men aware that gender is as important to us as it is to women."

Men start comprehending the issues when they see women and girls that they love facing discrimination. When men become fathers of girls, they often become instant feminists, says Kimmel. And research suggests male CEOs with daughters run more socially responsible firms.

## Tackle Resistance

The second obstacle is men's sense of entitlement, which leads to the resistance from those who believe handing over power means they lose, says Kimmel.

"Without confronting men's sense of entitlement, we will never understand why so many men resist gender equality. [It is] because we grew up thinking this is a level playing field and any policy that tilts it a little bit, we think it is reverse discrimination against us.

"Let me be really clear. White men in Australia, North America and Europe are the beneficiaries of the single greatest affirmative action program in the history of the world. It is called the history of the world."

## Make the Business Case

Kimmel says men need to understand and believe the business case for gender equality: that companies that are more gender equal have a high rate of return on investment, higher profitability, lower labour costs, lower turnover, higher job satisfaction and lower levels of absenteeism.

"These are all easily calculable labour costs," he says. "What we know is not only is gender equality right and fair and just, but we also know that it is smart. That it is good business."

Men need to understand that gender equality does not mean they "get less of the pie", but that the pie gets bigger. "It is not a zero sum game," said Kimmel.

## Make it Personal

Men need convincing that gender equality is good for them on an individual level—and that can start with their home life.

Kimmel points to research that shows when men share housework and childcare, their children do better at school, they have higher rates of achievement, lower rates of absenteeism, are less likely to be diagnosed with ADHD and childhood depression, less likely to see therapists and to be put on medication.

At the same time, their wives are happier, healthier, less likely to go to a therapist or be put on prescription medication, less likely to be diagnosed with depression, more likely to go the gym and they report higher levels of marital satisfaction.

When they do their fair share at home, men themselves are also happier and healthier. "They smoke less, they drink less, they take recreational drugs less often, they are more likely to go to doctors for routine screenings, but they are less likely to go to the emergency room, go to a therapist, take medication."

Focusing on the benefits of equality at home, says Kimmel, can be the start of changing attitudes to gender equality in the workplace, and everywhere else.

> *"You need to be open to the possibility that your experience of the world as a male/straight/white/cisgendered/ abled/documented/educated/etc./ etc. person might miss out on some of the struggles experienced by your less privileged planetmates."*

# Those Who Have Privilege Are Often Blind to It

**Chelsea Link**

*In the following viewpoint, Chelsea Link acknowledges that privilege is an emotionally charged topic and that it is hard to have rational conversations about it. Attempting to cut through the clutter as a person of privilege herself, Link calls for a heightened sensitivity to those with less privilege by those who benefit from society's invisible advantages. A key problem with privilege is that those who benefit from it are often blind to it. But privilege still must be acknowledged. The history of patriarchy has done much to instill men with privilege, and this history now limits how they should speak and act. Chelsea Link is the campus organizing fellow at the Humanist Community at Harvard. She has served as the vice president of outreach of the Harvard Secular Society and the president of the Harvard College Interfaith Council.*

"The Blindness of Privilege," by Chelsea Link, Patheos, May 24, 2013. Reprinted by permission.

As you read, consider the following questions:

1. Why does the author give the benefit of the doubt to those blind to privilege?
2. Why is calling someone out as privileged usually not helpful?
3. How does placing the idea of privilege in historical perspective advance Link's argument?

P rivilege is real, and it is a problem. This is a plea for us all to have better conversations about it.

I think I'm in a decent position to talk about this. After all, I am one of the most privileged people I know. I graduated from Harvard one year ago today. I've gotten sunburnt while skiing, which is probably the whitest sentence in the English language. I once got a concert grand harp for my birthday—my twelfth birthday. I've basically been deep-throating a silver spoon for 23 years.

In that time, I've had a lot of uncomfortable conversations about race, class, power, and privilege. I used to dismiss the people who used these words because none of them made sense to me and my experience. But I've had my eyes and ears opened a lot in recent years. I came to college, I met different kinds of people, I studied different things from different angles—the usual liberal agenda. I have a lot left to learn, but I've come to take the issue of privilege very seriously.

It's an issue that comes up a lot in the secular "movement" nowadays—Richard Dawkins is swimming in it yet oblivious to it, Jen McCreight tried to start a whole new movement to deal with it—but a lot of people are still sort of staring blankly and wondering what is going on and when they can go back to debating the atheology of Firefly.

So as somebody who can relate both to the people who see privilege everywhere and to those who don't get what everybody's whining about, I want to help translate so we can communicate more clearly. First, everybody's going to need to sit down and stop yelling and actually listen for a while, so go ahead and emotionally prepare yourself for that and come back when you're ready to be an adult about this.

Good? Good.

Let's start with something we all agree on: Facebook comment threads can be frustrating. Some extra-frustrating recent incidents pushed me over some kind of edge, which is why I'm here blogging after basically giving up on the Internet as a concept.

The other day, I posted a status update about how I'm planning on getting a second tattoo soon. An acquaintance of mine, a middle-aged man, shared some very well-meaning advice about how I should think about my future and remember that ink is permanent, and mentioned how glad he is that his 20s self had the foresight to remain unadorned. I retorted that I'd been wishing more men would tell me how my body should look, and pointed out that I know plenty of people of all ages who are satisfied with their choices of whether and how to modify their bodies. He then sent me a hurt and defensive message calling my "unfair" response a "cheap shot" and insisting that "gender has absolutely nothing to do with it."

A couple weeks earlier, I shared an article about the enshrinement of slut-shaming in school dress codes. It got some comments, including a lot of agreement as well as some respectful and thoughtful alternative opinions; all good so far. But it also evoked a lot of outright dismissal. Here follow some excerpts from real comments by real men—men whom Facebook labels my "friends," no less.

"I'm not seeing it." "I couldn't figure out what I was supposed to be offended by." "That anyone thinks that schools are out of line for outlawing clothes that are, in most cases, made with the explicit purpose of looking sexy is laughable." "And don't tell me that an extra 3 inches off of a skirt helps you keep cool." "What a bunch of nonsense." "Not to be condescending, but [condescending rant]." "This whole thing is so silly." "I don't think it's symptomatic of the 'rape culture.'" "It's just a damn dress code."

Here's the deal. If somebody of a different gender than yours says gender matters in a situation, it probably matters. Just because you don't see something (yet) doesn't mean it isn't there, and all your condescending, laughing, and scare-quoting will neither help you see it nor make what I see disappear. If lots of people with some common experience that you lack—a gender, an ethnicity, whatever—are all upset by something you don't even see, chances are better that you're facing the wrong way than that it simply doesn't exist.

You need to be open to the possibility that your experience of the world as a male/straight/white/cisgendered/abled/documented/educated/etc./etc. person might miss out on some of the struggles experienced by your less privileged planetmates. You need to admit that this might mean they know some things you don't and put up with some s*** you don't. You need to respect them and listen to them and take them seriously, not mansplain to them that their subjective experiences are incorrect.

One of the main problems with privilege is that usually the people who have it are nearly blind to it. I believe that this blindness exists not because privileged people are stupid or careless, but because its effects are nearly invisible to them by the very nature of the systems that make those people privileged in the first place. I think the majority of privileged people are smart, well-meaning, and compassionate, so let's give them the benefit of the doubt and assume they are not trying to ruin everything. They just don't know any better (yet).

As I said at the beginning, I know from experience that these kinds of ideas can be startling and disorienting to those of us lucky enough to be shielded from a lot of what goes on in the world. It's okay to feel that way, but it's not okay to use that as an excuse to abandon the conversation. When it comes to privilege, out of sight cannot mean out of mind.

So how are we going to get people to care about a phenomenon that doesn't even seem real to them? I think the biggest thing here is that calling someone out for privilege can't be a criminal accusation or a public shaming. Allow me to cast the first stone at myself: I should have found a less snarky way to point out the problematic aspects of the tattoo comment. I don't think my response was "unfair" or unduly harsh, but it was less helpful than it could have been. Yes, privilege is upsetting, but if we start by hurling epithets, people won't want to stick around to hear what else we have to say. When communication begins with an attack, the automatic response is to be defensive, not to listen. (See: all of atheism ever.)

Finally, one other comment on the dress code thread wasn't overtly offensive but did illustrate a mistake that perfectly nice smart privileged people tend to make: "I maintain that one could craft a similar or identical policy divorced from history, and thus the policy itself is not sexist."

That might be true, but last I checked, history was still waiting for its Henry VIII to come; for the foreseeable future, divorce isn't an option. This issue of inescapable histories of oppression is discussed in an excellent blog post on Brute Reason called "Why You Shouldn't Tell That Random Girl On The Street That She's Hot." This is a really fantastically good article and you should definitely read the entire thing, plus as many of the outlinks as you have time for. For now we'll focus on this part:

> In a perfect world, you could tell a woman she's hot and she would smile and say thank you because there would be no millennia-long history of women's bodies being used and abused by men, no notion of women's beauty as being "for" men, no ridiculous beauty standards. Complimenting a woman on her appearance would be just like complimenting a person on their bike or their shoes or the color of their hair; it would not carry all the baggage that it carries in this world.
>
> But that's not our world, and it may never be. Yeah, it sucks that women often take it "the wrong way" when you give them unsolicited compliments. You know what sucks more? Yup, patriarchy.

The fact is that there is no way to magically remove yourself from history; you are embedded in oppressive systems no matter what. Just because you don't see how a comment or action or policy relates to power dynamics and histories of oppression, that does not somehow make it officially neutral and vindicate you from any responsibility for perpetuating those systems. This means that there is no such thing as a neutral comment about a woman's body, about race, about same-sex attractions, about non-conforming genders, etc.

There is no neutral way for a school board to police the sexualities of its female students. There is no neutral way for a man to comment on an unknown woman's appearance. There is no neutral way for an older man to give me advice about my body modifications.

You are a part of the system whether or not you like it and whether or not you believe in it, so either you can join the resistance or you can sell your soul to The Man. Your choice.

> *"It is true that 'check your privilege'*
> *could offer sometimes-useful*
> *reminders to think carefully and*
> *empathetically about others'*
> *circumstances, which may be far*
> *different than ours. But it can bear*
> *good fruit only as the beginning of a*
> *far deeper open discussion. Yet that*
> *has not been the result."*

# Privilege Rhetoric Squelches Discourse

### Gary M. Galles

*In the following viewpoint, Gary M. Galles finds fault with privilege checks, in which an offended party instructs another to "check your privilege." Such admonitions may have validity, but as they are currently used, they are simply a way for the offended party to declare victory rather than open a dialogue about the offense. He notes that the explicit rationale of those asking another to check your privilege is to advance public discussion but actually has the effect of shutting down dialogue and undermining social cooperation. Gary M. Galles is a professor of economics at Pepperdine University. His recent books include* Faulty Premises, Faulty Policies, *and* Apostle of Peace.

As you read, consider the following questions:

1. Does the claim that there is no truth to the concerns of those who ask others to check their privilege have validity? Explain.
2. How does this disagreement boil down to a battle between liberals and conservatives?
3. What, according to the viewpoint, would be more useful than the privilege check?

Recently, I came across an article from conservative author Derek Hunter (most recent book: *Outrage, Inc.*) titled "It's Time For A Serious Conversation About Serious Conversations," which I found very insightful. The core of his argument was:

> Democrats … insist, loudly and often, that "it's time the nation has a serious conversation" about whatever they're claiming is the most important thing at that time. Weirdly, they never have that conversation, on any topic. At least not with anyone who has a different perspective from them.

Hunter put useful words to what I had inchoately sensed. And he did a good job of using assertions of racism as an almost ubiquitous example of shutting down any kind of serious conversation while claiming the need to have one.

However, I think there may be an even clearer example of the cognitive dissonance Hunter refers to—suggestions that you should "check your privilege" before offering an opinion someone else doesn't like, which has become a mainstay of social justice rhetoric and the presumption behind a bumper crop of microaggression accusations. The explicit rationale offered by practitioners is to advance public discussion, while its use has been to squelch it.

## The Problem with "Check Your Privilege" Rhetoric

Those unleashing "check your privilege" barrages describe them as reminders to always be empathetic and sensitive to others' feelings. A gentle version is that you (but never them) might be including some inappropriate assumptions behind your conclusions. Something that may be sensible for you, given your asserted privilege, may not be sensible for others, and the ensuing misunderstanding can lead to insufficient consideration of others and erroneous evaluations.

Of course, the demanded sensitivity also awards anyone asserting hurt feelings unilateral veto power over your ability to share or defend what you believe.

By defining you as outside the oppressed class, it also "justifies" treating you as part of the oppressor class. And putting that label on you means objectors need not listen to, much less respect, your arguments. Further, your inherent "wrongness" as an oppressor sacrifices your rights and property to satisfy anyone defining themselves as oppressed.

How can we tell if applications of such "logic" advance serious discussions and better social relations or do violence to the possibility? Ask what would be entailed if "check your privilege" was intended to advance such a conversation.

When such terms are used to preemptively cut off communication by stopping those who disagree from being heard or taken seriously, neither clarity nor empathy will be improved. So such assertions must not end discussions; they must facilitate more complete conversations.

As actually used, "check your privilege" is an assertion that you are wrong in your understanding and views—and too self-absorbed to notice. However, it leaves how and why unspecified beyond membership in an allegedly privileged group defined by accusers. Progress toward better understanding requires several additional steps.

# The Problem with Identity Politics

The idea that all white people systemically benefit from the colour of their skin, and in turn oppress people of a different skin tone, is a myth in opposition to the liberal ideal of individuality over group identity. The Gold Trail School District has decided that the colour of one's skin is enough to make assumptions about one's personal circumstances and access to opportunity. It is the narrative of the oppressor and oppressed; that white people have systemic privilege in western society at the expense of others and should feel guilty for it. The message is deeply divisive, drawing a distinction between students on the basis of skin colour instead of their individual merit. So much for Martin Luther King's dream.

It's concerning to think where this could go. Public figures have already begun to openly use identity politics to try and suppress others' rights to freedom of conscience and freedom of speech. Senator Katy Gallagher attempted to dismiss challenges made by Mitch Fifield on the basis of his gender, making allusions to his privileged identity as a male. Canadian MP Celina Caesar-Chavannes deployed similar tactics, directing fellow MP Maxime Bernier to "Please check your privilege and be quiet". These are people in power who believe some people are more entitled to opinion and authority than others on the basis of group identity. What could happen in schools? Will we start to treat students perceived to be oppressed—people of colour, women, indigenous peoples etc.—differently to those considered privileged? Will people in power begin to afford them special rights?

Identity politics is a slippery slope. We should hold true to our liberal ideals so perfectly captured in I Have A Dream and actively speak out against this slide towards division on the basis of identity. That society is beginning to underestimate the importance of judging people as individuals is a big problem. But society imposing this on our young people? That's a huge concern.

It needs to stop. Now.

"Keep the Myth of White Privilege out of Our Schools," by John Kenny, March 10, 2018. https://johnkennyweb.wordpress.com/2018/03/10/keep-the-myth-of-white-privilege-out-of-our-schools/

## Refusing to Acknowledge Your Argument

Progress would require specifying precisely what faulty premises, assumptions, or arguments a person holds, as well as why they are inappropriate for the issues considered. The appropriate premises to replace them would then need articulation and rational responses to objections.

How the "new and improved" premises would alter one's conclusions would need demonstration followed by considering the appropriate remedies based on the alternative analysis. It would have to explain how proposed remedies were not merely "more for me" gambits connected to the rationales offered only by self-interest.

It would have to justify any special privileges to be created for those claiming victimhood status, including any coercive impositions on others required to create them.

It is true that "check your privilege" could offer sometimes-useful reminders to think carefully and empathetically about others' circumstances, which may be far different than ours. But it can bear good fruit only as the beginning of a far deeper open discussion. Yet that has not been the result.

The phrase, as actually used, has been to peremptorily declare victory in social justice disputes, assert special privileges for those self-defined as morally superior due to oppression, and disqualify those who disagree from any consideration, without any coherent argument.

That social demonization is repeatedly employed trying to leverage coercive imposition of "solutions" at the expense of those they decide must make it up to them. That, in turn, undermines social cooperation by undermining the rights upon which it is built without advancing understanding or empathy.

> *"What outrages people is not the single jokes of a single comedian; it is the pervasive discrimination that comes to light through these jokes. The problem is not a comedian making a racist or sexist joke, the problem is a racist and sexist society that puts him on prime time and laughs along with him."*

# Laughing at Privilege

*Rocio Ros Rebollo*

*In the following viewpoint, Rocio Ros Rebollo argues that comedy targeting oppressed groups is outdated. The author spotlights feminist comedians who successfully use humor to speak truth to power. She makes the point that there is confusion about comedy in this age of political correctness. Some comedians claim that you can't make a joke without offending somebody. However, the author points out, the problem isn't about making jokes about oppressed groups, but rather the position the comedian is coming from. Comedians should consider their places of privilege before firing. Rocio Ros Rebollo is a Spanish journalist and entrepreneur. Her startup, Proyecto V, is a digital magazine specializing in feminist journalism.*

As you read, consider the following questions:

1. How did supporters of the comedian mentioned at the beginning of the viewpoint defend him?
2. How can humor marginalize people, according to the viewpoint?
3. How do some feminist comics manage to find humor in oppressed groups?

This summer, an old debate broke out again in Spain: should we put limits on humour? This time it was prompted by a monologue from comedian Rober Bodegas in which he mocked gypsies that steal cars, don't know how to write, and marry 13-years-old girls.

The comedian was accused of racism by gypsy people, whereas some of his colleagues defended him, arguing that humour's purpose is to provoke and transgress social rules. Even if Bodegas was laughing at archaic stereotypes, they said, people should have taken it with humour and as a simple joke.

After receiving more than 400 death threats, according to Bodegas, and thousands of angry comments on Twitter, he apologised and the video of his monologue was removed – but the questions it raised remain live.

Jorge Cremades previously provoked a similar debate. He became famous with comic videos featuring a raft of sexist clichés. On Facebook, he has seven million followers. In June 2017, feminist groups asked people to boycott his show at a Barcelona theatre, calling him "macho and patriarchal".

What's the right answer? Should we stop making or ban jokes about groups that experience discrimination, or should we give comedians complete freedom to laugh at whatever and whoever they'd like?

According to presenter and comedian David Broncano, jokes can't be limited as there will always be someone offended by them.

I understand his point: censuring some topics is contrary to the transgressive nature of humour.

But who says we must censure topics? When oppressed groups react against a joke, it doesn't mean they want to put up limits in humour. The demand is rather that comedians bear in mind from which position are they making these jokes, and understand the effect of such a powerful weapon as humour.

## "Such a powerful weapon"

Humour is instrumental. That is, it can serve different purposes depending on how we use it. Usually we think about it as a way to make someone crack up by destroying social rules, but it can be used to marginalise people too.

"Who are the protagonists of most jokes? People that are excluded… Humour is used also to put people in [their] place", said Asunción Bernárdez, director of the Instituto de Investigaciones Feministas, earlier this year.

In other words: when a comedian laughs at discriminated groups from a privileged position, what he is doing is re-emphasising difference and relativising the oppression that these groups suffer.

What outrages people is not the single jokes of a single comedian; it is the pervasive discrimination that comes to light through these jokes. The problem is not a comedian making a racist or sexist joke, the problem is a racist and sexist society that puts him on prime time and laughs along with him.

When you understand the violence behind humour that, using the excuse of being transgressive, plays with racism, sexism or homophobia, it starts to provoke anger instead of laughter. And you realise that making fun of oppressed people is the least transgressive thing you can do.

Against easy humour that uses stereotypes to laugh at others, the feminist writer Brigitte Vasallo proposes to "point inside or to point up"—and laugh about yourself or those who are more powerful than you.

This is not utopian; there are already feminist comedians that can make you cry with laughter like Patricia Sornosa, Ali Wong or Tig Notaro. And some of them talk about minorities and oppressed groups too.

"If there was an Oppression Olympics, I would win the gold medal. I'm Palestinian, Muslim, I'm female, I'm disabled... and I live in New Jersey," is how actor Maysoon Zayid starts I got 99 problems and palsy is just one.

Zayid can make fun of her conditions and express irony that is actually empowering. This is what feminist humour is about.

Making fun of the privileged is not new for Spanish comedians who openly mock governments and establishments. But most are men who seem to have forgotten to laugh about themselves— and patriarchy.

Artist Lula Gómez commented on this in one of her feminist videos called "Eres una caca" (You are poop): "Maybe unconsciously, maybe not, but they aren't able to make jokes about their own privileges as men".

Some people might not agree with my analysis. At least, you should agree with me that humour consists of distorting reality and, to do this, we need to start from the same reality, from the same common point.

When we make a joke, we must take into account the social context in which we make it, and we know that a lot of people are still discriminated against in our reality. That should be our common starting point.

# Periodical and Internet Sources Bibliography

*The following articles have been selected to supplement the diverse views presented in this chapter.*

Charles Blow, "Checking My Male Privilege." *New York Times.* Oct. 29, 2017. https://www.nytimes.com/2017/10/29/opinion/checking-my-male-privilege.html

Max Boot, "2017 Was the Year I Learned About My White Privilege." *Foreign Policy.* Dec. 27, 2017. https://foreignpolicy.com/2017/12/27/2017-was-the-year-i-learned-about-my-white-privilege/

Phoebe Maltz Bovy, "The Perils of "Privilege" *New Republic.* March 6, 2017. https://newrepublic.com/article/140985/perils-privilege-phoebe-maltz-bovy-book-excerpt

Amy Chua "How America's identity politics went from inclusion to division." *The Guardian.* Mar. 1 2018. https://www.theguardian.com/society/2018/mar/01/how-americas-identity-politics-went-from-inclusion-to-division

Daniel Cubias, "Let's Get Rid of the Term 'White Privilege'" Huffington Post. July 7, 2015. https://www.huffingtonpost.com/daniel-cubias/lets-get-rid-of-the-term-white-privilege_b_7835872.html

Sam Dylan Finch, "Ever Been Told to 'Check Your Privilege?' Here's What That Really Means." Everyday Feminism. July 27, 2015. https://everydayfeminism.com/2015/07/what-checking-privilege-means/

Tal Fortgang, "Why I'll Never Apologize for My White Privilege." *Time.* May 2, 2014. http://time.com/85933/why-ill-never-apologize-for-my-white-male-privilege/

Gabby Hinsloff, "'Check your privilege' used to annoy me. Now I get it." *Guardian.* Dec. 27, 2017. https://www.theguardian.com/commentisfree/2017/dec/27/check-your-privilege-racism-sexism-education-income

Michael Karson, "The Privilege of Not Understanding Privilege." Feb 13, 2017. https://www.psychologytoday.com/us/blog/feeling-our-way/201702/the-privilege-not-understanding-privilege

Brianna Payton, "Dear Privileged-at-Princeton: You. Are. Privileged. And Meritocracy Is a Myth." *Time.* May 6, 2014. http://time. com/89482/dear-privileged-at-princeton-you-are-privileged-and-meritocracy-is-a-myth/

W. Bradford Wilcox, "2.5 Million Black Men Are in the Upper Class." July 23, 2018. https://ifstudies.org/blog/2-5-million-black-men-are-in-the-upper-class

Joanna Williams, "No, I Won't Check My Privilege." *American Conservative.* May 25, 2018. https://www. theamericanconservative.com/articles/no-i-wont-check-my-privilege/

**OPPOSING
VIEWPOINTS®
SERIES**

# CHAPTER 2

# What Does White Privilege Mean?

# Chapter Preface

Any discussion of white privilege must acknowledge Peggy McIntosh's groundbreaking work. As a white feminist, McIntosh was investigating the inequities between men and women when she realized that she, herself, was benefiting from a system designed to favor those with her own skin color. Her now famous examples of white privilege include everything from turning on the television to see people who resemble oneself to buying Band-Aids that match one's skin color. McIntosh's writing set up a new debate on race that has continued and only expanded in the last several decades.

White privilege manifests itself in so many other ways in our society. When white drivers are stopped by a police officer, for the most part they can safely assume that they will not be harassed or treated unfairly. Such has not always been the case for black drivers. As journalist Max Boot wrote, "For African-Americans, and in particular African-American men, infractions like jaywalking or speeding or selling cigarettes without tax stamps can incite corporal, or even capital, punishment without benefit of judge or jury." Thus the expression "Driving While Black" has been coined as a satirical comment on how black motorists are more likely to be targeted by police officers. Sandra Bland, an African-American woman from Chicago, was arrested in rural Texas after a police officer pulled her over for failing to signal, and the confrontation escalated. Bland later committed suicide after spending three days in jail.

Another high profile case was that of Trayvon Martin, a seventeen-year-old African American boy who was walking home from a convenience store with Skittles in one hand and an Arizona fruit juice in the other when he was confronted by neighborhood watch captain George Zimmerman, who after a skirmish, shot him to death. Like the officer in the Sandra Bland case, Zimmerman was never convicted of a crime in the incident.

These violations of the rights of African Americans, along with the shooting deaths of unarmed black males such as Tamar Rice in Ohio; Philando Castile in Minnesota; Alton Sterling in Louisiana; and perhaps most famously, Michael Brown Jr. in Ferguson, Missouri, have fueled the controversial Black Lives Matter movement, created in response to the murder of Trayvon Martin. Their mission "is to build local power and to intervene in violence inflicted on Black communities by the state and vigilantes."

But the movement has sparked controversy and backlash, particularly after National Football League Players such as Colin Kaepernick picked up the mantle and began protesting police brutality against African Americans. Critics, such as author Steve Salerno, claim that the number of black deaths at the hands of the police is overblown: "In 2017, American cops killed 19 unarmed blacks. There are 30 million blacks over age 18 living in America. The 19 killings thus represented a death rate of .00000063333—less than one ten-thousandth of 1 percent. Nothing can be deduced from a sample that small," he wrote in Quillette in 2018. Salerno believes that the Black Lives Matter movement is fueled by media hype and paranoia.

Despite the pushback, an increasing awareness of white privilege has generated valuable discussions in the United States and abroad about how the power structure systematically oppresses marginalized populations. The viewpoints in this chapter present a wide range of opinions on white privilege, Black Lives Matter, and related subjects.

| "A bias against minorities runs rampant through the resume screening process at companies throughout the United States."

# Minorities Who "Whiten" Résumés Get More Job Interviews

*Dina Gerdeman*

*In the following viewpoint Dina Gerdeman writes that US businesses have an ingrained racial bias even when they claim not to. A research study reveals that minorities who avoid racial clues on their résumés are more likely to be interviewed. Even when companies claim to be pro-diversity or equal opportunity employers, the study shows that they still discriminate against minority applicants. But minorities are more likely to include racial clues in résumés when they see these philosophies, adding to their disadvantage. Given these realities, businesses must address discriminatory hiring processes. Dina Gerdeman is a freelance writer and editor living in the Boston area. She covers business news and features.*

"Minorities Who 'Whiten' Job Resumes Get More Interviews," by Dina Gerdeman, President & Fellows of Harvard College, May 17, 2017. Reprinted by permission.

As you read, consider the following questions:

1. Why does the researcher in this article not believe that diversity statements are a "set-up" to identify minority applicants?
2. How are minority applicants "whitening" résumés?
3. How can businesses address discriminatory hiring processes?

Minority job applicants are "whitening" their resumes by deleting references to their race with the hope of boosting their shot at jobs, and research shows the strategy is paying off.

In fact, companies are more than twice as likely to call minority applicants for interviews if they submit whitened resumes than candidates who reveal their race—and this discriminatory practice is just as strong for businesses that claim to value diversity as those that don't.

These research findings should provide a startling wakeup call for business executives: A bias against minorities runs rampant through the resume screening process at companies throughout the United States, says Katherine A. DeCelles, the James M. Collins Visiting Associate Professor of Business Administration at Harvard Business School.

"Discrimination still exists in the workplace," DeCelles says. "Organizations now have an opportunity to recognize this issue as a pinch point, so they can do something about it."

DeCelles co-authored a September 2016 article about the two-year study in Administrative Science Quarterly called Whitened Resumes: Race and Self-Presentation in the Labor Market with Sonia K. Kang, assistant professor of organizational behavior and human resource management at the University of Toronto Mississauga; András Tilcsik, assistant professor of strategic management at the University of Toronto; and Sora Jun, a doctoral candidate at Stanford University.

## WHITE PRIVILEGE IS STILL A PROBLEM

If you are a white person in America, you were born privileged. That's just a fact.

It's nothing to be ashamed of. It's not anybody's fault. There's no need to get defensive about it.

The best thing to do is just acknowledge it.

Being privileged does not necessarily mean that you have a perfect life. It does not mean that you come from wealth or that you always obtain everything you want—or deserve.

It just means that you have a head start over the rest of us.

White privilege means that you were born with an inherent advantage over every other race of people. The whiteness of your skin alone allows you to leave the starting gate quicker and to run the race with fewer obstacles. White skin comes with certain other perks, too, many of which are taken for granted.

American culture itself is white-centric. For example, as an African-American woman, I can rarely find makeup that matches my exact skin tone. Though cosmetics companies have gotten a lot better at adding more diverse colors to their lines, I still most often have to buy two shades and mix them together to get a match.

In one study, the researchers created resumes for black and Asian applicants and sent them out for 1,600 entry-level jobs posted on job search websites in 16 metropolitan sections of the United States. Some of the resumes included information that clearly pointed out the applicants' minority status, while others were whitened, or scrubbed of racial clues. The researchers then created email accounts and phone numbers for the applicants and observed how many were invited for interviews.

Employer callbacks for resumes that were whitened fared much better in the application pile than those that included ethnic information, even though the qualifications listed were identical. Twenty-five percent of black candidates received callbacks from their whitened resumes, while only 10 percent got calls when they left ethnic details intact. Among Asians, 21 percent got calls if they

> If you were born white, you are likely to earn more money than an African-American or Hispanic co-worker who does the same work. You are more likely to be considered for a promotion than a racial minority who is just as qualified. Numerous studies back this up.
>
> But the perception many white people have about other white people—whether it is conscious or subconscious—is that they are smarter, more ambitious, more dependable and harder working than African-Americans.
>
> Black and brown people have no reason to be angry with white people for being born white. We don't buy into the adage that because someone happened to be white, they are smarter than the rest of us. Nor do we believe that every white person seated at the head table deserves a space there.
>
> What we do understand is that white skin opens doors that often slam shut in the faces of dark skin. That's what we have a problem with.
>
> The reality is that blacks and Latinos have never gotten an equal shake. When affirmative action sought to level the playing field, white people got mad and put an end to it.
>
> **"Yes, White 'Privilege' Is Still the Problem," by Dahleen Glanton, New Century Foundation, March 29, 2018.**

used whitened resumes, whereas only 11.5 percent heard back if they sent resumes with racial references.

## "Pro-Diversity" Employers Discriminate, Too

What's worse for minority applicants: When an employer says it values diversity in its job posting by including words like "equal opportunity employer" or "minorities are strongly encouraged to apply," many minority applicants get the false impression that it's safe to reveal their race on their resumes—only to be rejected later.

In one study to test whether minorities whiten less often when they apply for jobs with employers that seem diversity-friendly, the researchers asked some participants to craft resumes for jobs that included pro-diversity statements and others to write resumes for jobs that didn't mention diversity.

They found minorities were half as likely to whiten their resumes when applying for jobs with employers who said they care about diversity. One black student explained in an interview that with each resume she sent out, she weighed whether to include her involvement in a black student organization: "If the employer is known for like trying to employ more people of color and having like a diversity outreach program, then I would include it because in that sense they're trying to broaden their employees, but if they're not actively trying to reach out to other people of other races, then no, I wouldn't include it."

But these applicants who let their guard down about their race ended up inadvertently hurting their chances of being considered: Employers claiming to be pro-diversity discriminated against resumes with racial references just as much as employers who didn't mention diversity at all in their job ads.

"This is a major point of our research—that you are at an even greater risk for discrimination when applying with a pro-diversity employer because you're being more transparent," DeCelles says. "Those companies have the same rate of discrimination, which makes you more vulnerable when you expose yourself to those companies."

DeCelles sees an obvious disconnect between the companies' pro-diversity messages and the actual acceptance of diverse applicants, yet she doesn't believe employers are using these messages as a way to trap and weed out minorities that do apply.

"I don't think it's intended to be a setup," she says. "These organizations are not necessarily all talk when they say they're pro-diversity. Maybe the diversity values are there, but they just haven't been translated from the person who writes the job ad to the person who is screening resumes."

But clearly the findings reinforce an assumption many minorities already have: that the resume screening game is stacked against them and that they need to hide their race to level the playing field.

The researchers interviewed 59 Asian and African American students between the ages of 18 and 25 who were seeking jobs and internships. More than a third, 36 percent, said they whiten their resumes, and two-thirds knew friends or family members who had done so, all because they were afraid their resumes could be unfairly tossed aside if their race became obvious.

"The primary concern is that were trying to avoid a negative group-based stereotype that they felt could occur in a quick scan of a resume," DeCelles says. "They whitened their resumes because they wanted to appear more mainstream."

## Different Minority Groups Use Different Whitening Techniques

Asian applicants often changed foreign-sounding names to something American-sounding—like substituting "Luke" for "Lei"—and they also "Americanized" their interests by adding outdoorsy activities like hiking, snowboarding, and kayaking that are common in white western culture.

One Asian applicant said she put her "very Chinese-sounding" name on her resume in her freshman year, but only got noticed after subbing in her American nickname later: "Before I changed it, I didn't really get any interviews, but after that I got interviews," she said.

Some Asians covered up their race because they worried employers might be concerned about a possible language barrier. "You can't prove your English is good in a resume scan, but you can if you can get to the interview," DeCelles says.

Meanwhile, African Americans toned down mentions of race from black organizations they belonged to, such as dropping the word "black" from a membership in a professional society for black engineers. Others omitted impressive achievements altogether, including one black college senior who nixed a prestigious scholarship from his resume because he feared it would reveal his race.

"Some applicants were willing to lose what could be seen as valuable pieces of human capital because they were more worried about giving away their race," DeCelles says.

Some black students bleached out this information because they were concerned they might come across as politically radical or tied to racially controversial causes in a way that could turn off an employer.

"People … want to have like an awesome black worker but they want one who they feel like fits within a certain box and like very much will conform and like lay low and just kind of do what's expected of them, and they're not necessarily looking for the outspoken like political radical person," a black college senior said. "I feel like race is just one of the many aspects where you try to just like buff the surface smooth … and pretend like there's nothing sticking out."

Other interviewed students were staunchly opposed to resume whitening. Some even said they purposely left in racial references as a way of sniffing out employers that might not welcome minorities. One student said, "If blackness put a shadow over all (my resume), then it probably isn't the job I want to be in," while another said, "I wouldn't consider whitening my resume because if they don't accept my racial identity, I don't see how I would fit in that job."

## How to Address Discriminatory Hiring Practices

It's time for employers to acknowledge that bias is hardwired into the hiring system and that prejudice is clouding the screening of qualified applicants, says DeCelles, whose research focuses on the intersection of organizational behavior and criminology.

Business leaders should start by taking a closer look at their resume screening processes. Blind recruitment is one possible solution, where information about race, age, gender, or social class are removed from resumes before hiring managers see them.

Companies can also perform regular checks for discrimination in the screening process, for example by measuring how many minorities applied for a position and comparing that with the percentage of those applicants who made the first cut.

"Organizations can now see very clearly that this is why they are not meeting their diversity goals," DeCelles says. "They can't just put a message on recruitment ads and be done. They need to follow through with a clear structure and staff training. They need to make goals and then continually evaluate the outcome in order to meet those goals."

The bottom line for business leaders who are hiring, she says: "Once you receive applications, you need to make sure they are evaluated fairly."

> *"No reasonable person can argue that white privilege applies to the great majority of whites, let alone to all whites. There are simply too many variables other than race that determine individual success in America."*

# White Privilege Is a Fallacy

*Dennis Prager*

*In the following viewpoint, Dennis Prager attacks what he considers the leftist notion of white privilege. Claiming that no reasonable person would argue that all whites are better off due to the color of their skin, Prager cites evidence against privilege theory, including statistics on white vs. black suicide, and the other privileges that "dwarf" white privilege. Prager believes that there are cases where minorities are privileged, such as in the college admissions process. For Prager, privilege theory is a progressive political idea that keeps minorities from working on active solutions to their problems. Dennis Prager is a radio talk-show host and columnist. He is the author of* The Rational Bible, *a commentary on the book of Exodus. He is the founder of Prager University.*

"The Fallacy of 'White Privilege,'" by Dennis Prager, National Review, February 16, 2016. Reprinted by permission.

As you read, consider the following questions:

1. How does Prager use white suicide rates in his argument?
2. What examples does Prager give to discount white privilege?
3. What are some examples of privilege that dwarf white privilege?

A pillar of contemporary Leftism is the notion of "white privilege." Given that a generation of high-school and college students are being taught that a great number of "unearned privileges" accrue to white Americans, the charge of white privilege demands rational inquiry.

The assertion turns out to be largely meaningless. And, more significantly, it does great harm to blacks.

First, no reasonable person can argue that white privilege applies to the great majority of whites, let alone to all whites. There are simply too many variables other than race that determine individual success in America.

And if it were true, why would whites commit suicide at twice the rate of blacks (and at a higher rate than any other race in America except American Indians)? According to the American Foundation for Suicide Prevention, white men, who the Left argues are the most privileged group of all in America, commit seven out of every ten suicides in America—even though only three out of ten Americans are white males.

Whatever reason one gives for the white suicide rate, it is indisputable that, at the very least, considerably more whites than blacks consider life not worth living. To argue that all these whites were oblivious to all the unique privileges they had is to stretch the definition of "privilege" beyond credulity.

Second, there are a host of privileges that dwarf "white privilege."

A huge one is Two-Parent Privilege. If you are raised by a father and mother, you enter adulthood with more privileges than anyone else in American society, irrespective of race, ethnicity, or sex. That's why the poverty rate among two-parent black families is only 7 percent.

Compare that with a 22 percent poverty rate among whites in single-parent homes. Obviously the two-parent home is the decisive "privilege."

Another "privilege," if one wants to use that term, that dwarfs "white privilege" is Asian privilege. Asian Americans do better than white Americans in school, on IQ tests, on credit scores, and on other positive measures. In fact, according to recent data from the Federal Reserve, Asians are about to surpass whites as the wealthiest group of Americans. Will the Left soon complain about Asian privilege?

And how about "gentile privilege?" For most of American history it was a lot easier being a Christian than being a Jew in America. Yet, I do not know a Jew—myself included—who doesn't believe that to be a Jew in America has always been an unbelievable stroke of good fortune. It is not surprising that an American Jew, Irving Berlin, wrote "God Bless America."

There are even times when there is "minority privilege" in America today.

Every high-school student knows that given similar scholastic and extra-curricular records, one's chances of being accepted into a prestigious college are considerably greater if one is a member of a minority, most especially the black minority.

And the biggest privilege of all is American privilege. Unless you or your family make some big mistakes, the greatest privilege of all is to be an American. That's why much of the world wants to live in America.

So then why all this left-wing talk about white privilege?

The major reason is in order to portray blacks as victims. This achieves two huge goals for the Left—one political, the other philosophical.

The political goal is to ensure that blacks continue to view America as racist. The Left knows that the only way to retain political power in America is to perpetuate the belief among black

Americans that their primary problem is white racism. Only then will blacks continue to regard the Left and the Democrats as indispensable.

The philosophical reason is that the Left denies—as it has since Marx—the primacy of moral and cultural values in determining the fate of the individual and of society. In the Left's view, it is not poor values or a lack of moral self-control that causes crime, but poverty and, in the case of black criminals, racism. Therefore, the disproportionate amount of violent crime committed by black males is not attributable to the moral failure of the black criminal or to the likelihood of his not having been raised by a father, but to an external factor over which he has little or no power—white racism.

White privilege is another left-wing attempt, and a successful one, to keep America from focusing on what will truly help black America—a resurrection of the black family, for example—and instead to focus on an external problem: white privilege.

In doing so, the Left has become the only real enemy the black has in America today.

> *"So to my growing list of white privileges I didn't realize I was enjoying, I add the freedom to not fear the police, the opportunity to respect them, the privilege to run right toward them if I need help, and to know for certain that they will."*

# Not Fearing the Police Is White Privilege in Action

## Heather M. Edwards

*In the following viewpoint Heather M. Edwards argues that until recently, she had never considered that some people do not think of interactions with law enforcement as potentially helpful or beneficial in any way. She had been raised in a military family and two of her cousins were deputy sheriffs. But examples of police brutality and police corruption have opened her eyes. She now understands that people of color have a very different relationship with law enforcement and that her ability to not fear the police is a form of white privilege. Heather M. Edwards blogs for sites such as Medium and the Writing Cooperative.*

"The White Privilege of Not Fearing the Police," by Heather M. Edwards, Medium.com, November 11, 2018. Reprinted by permission.

As you read, consider the following questions:

1. Why did Edwards not realize that some people feared interactions with the police?
2. How does Edwards make use of her friend Monica Froman-Reid's insights?
3. What is Edwards's new attitude toward law enforcement?

When I wrote about the 7 White Privileges I Didn't Realize I Was Enjoying I acknowledged that there are probably even more than seven that I'm still not aware of. It made me realize that one of the most intrinsic characteristics of privilege is not realizing you're privileged. It doesn't automatically mean that you're racist. But it does mean you could be benefitting from your skin color without realizing it.

Which brings me to our boys in blue.

If you're white, chances are seeing a police officer fills you with one of two things: relief or gratitude. If you see them coming and you're in distress you probably enjoy the privilege of immediate relief. If you are not in distress and see them coming you probably give them one slow nod of gratitude or a smiling greeting. Or if you're my (white) friend Pamela, ask if you can buy them coffee. It never occurred to me that anyone would feel anything but admiration for their rigorous training, long hours, the requisite danger and risk and the time away from their families. Because I have only had positive experiences with law enforcement.

My friend, psychologist Dr. Monica Froman-Reid is as sharp as she is compassionate.

> People often struggle with empathy when it is not something they or their family members have had to experience. Check out the Helms White Identity Model for more insight into those who identify as "color blind". Additionally many folks adhere to a just world fallacy (check out Lerner's social psychology research) and don't want to accept that bad things can happen to people randomly and with no fault of their own. If you are

## EXPLAINING WHITE MALE PRIVILEGE TO A PRIVILEGED WHITE MALE

I've never felt privileged.

I've worked my ass off my whole life.

When I hear that some fraction of what I have is due to privilege, and not due to hard work, my defenses go up. And I discredit the notion. And the person using the phrase. And I get pissed.

I was on a business trip with my boss. Brilliant engineer. Even better leader. Empowering, vulnerable, made me feel like a partner rather than an employee. The whole package.

Also, black.

We'd arrived at our destination and were at a convenience store to pick up a few things. We'd each paid by credit card. Walking out, he has this slight smirk on his face.

"What's up?" I ask.

"I always have to show ID when I use my credit card," he says. "Not this time. Guess I need to bring you with me more often."

I don't really believe him. Coincidence, I think.

Same business trip. Same boss. Bar across the parking lot from the hotel. We'd planned to meet there to review some last-minute changes to the presentation we were making the next day.

I walk in. He's waiting at a table, no drink. I sit down across from him. Bartender comes over. Takes our order. Leaves.

in a position of privilege, it can be threatening to acknowledge that society is not equitable.

But if you're Black or any non-white POC I've learned that the relationship with law enforcement can be anything from strained to fatal. That's right. I am 40 years old and I absolutely did not know that until recently.

I almost 100% attribute this shocking revelation to social media. Were it not for Black Lives Matter and the advocacy around racial justice I simply would not have known that other people had a drastically different experience with and relationship to law enforcement.

Again, the slight smirk.

"Now what?" I ask.

He glances at his watch. "I've been here 10 minutes."

I believe him a little more. Still, coincidence.

Same business trip. Same boss. Meeting with our vendor. They don't know us, don't know who's in charge.

He walks into the conference room slightly ahead of me. They shake my hand first. They're talking to me.

"I don't know, what do you think, boss?" I ask, glancing at him.

Slight smirk.

I believe him.

I can't concentrate for the rest of the meeting. Thinking about it all. He handles everything.

Same business trip. Same boss. Same bar.

He opens up.

It's like riding a bike. You ever start out riding a bike with the wind behind you? How much do you notice that tailwind? You don't. But what happens when you turn around to go home? Then you notice. You had no idea you even had a tailwind until it became a headwind. You never notice the tailwind.

Brilliant engineer. Even better leader.

Doing it all with a headwind.

**"The best way to explain white male privilege to a privileged white male." by Chris Sowers, Medium.com, June 10, 2018.**

I'll admit, the first time I saw an All Lives Matter meme, a matte black background with a thin blue line behind the text, it resonated. I am almost positive I reposted it on my page. So for everyone who says it's a waste of time to argue politics on facebook and that nobody changes their minds based on social media, just know that there is always the possibility that a naive but open-minded white woman can change. Exposure can be tremendously educational and social media is a far-reaching opportunity to touch people with the stories that aren't being told. I didn't know my worldview was loosely defined by the Just-World Hypothesis, nor had I even I even heard of it until Monica posted about it. I have since changed my mind based on innumerable cell phone posts of atrocious and vicious police brutality all over my country—the land of the free. And as has been heartbreakingly pointed out, it's not new, it's just being filmed now.

I grew up in the military. Many people close to me are military. My favorite uncle was a career firefighter. Two of my cousins are deputy sheriffs. I get to associate the uniform with the integrity of these people that I know and love.

I think about the cops who came to my childhood home when we got robbed, the deputy who found my car when it was stolen, the cop who pulled me over afterward because my car was still in their database as stolen, the cop who let me go with a warning when I was talking on my cell phone the day after it became illegal while driving, and the nice cop I did a ride-along with for a middle school project. Not only has my dignity always been respected in these interactions, but every interaction I have had with law enforcement bolstered my sense of safety. I felt protected and I felt tremendous respect for their bravery.

I smile when I see them walking toward me. They always say hi to me if I haven't already said hello first. And I have had the same experience in other cities in the US, as well as in Kenya, Turkey, Mexico and South Korea.

"Did you ever think it might be because you're white?" a Mexican friend asked me during the Ferguson protests. Reeling, I was telling him how well I'd always been treated by police. I was shocked by all the anti-police outrage. "And tiny and female and 'non-threatening'?"

I hadn't.

There are the hometown heroes like Officer Chris Kilcullen who was killed in my hometown at a routine traffic stop gone terribly wrong. There are pictures of him taped to espresso machines all over Dutch Bros. drive-thru coffee stands. He was apparently adored by all, including the baristas all over town where he would feed his need for caffeine. The college kids who worked at these coffee stands knew him and loved him. One of them showed me their picture of him while we waited for my mocha. He was unashamed as he wiped tears away.

I didn't know Officer Kilcullen. But on my way home from work I happened by a memorial that was taking place for him. An American flag was stretched and suspended between the ladders of two firetrucks. He had a wife and two young children. I parked and stood on the sidewalk crying without caring.

But there are also cops from the second circle of hell like Roger "Officer Blowjob" Magaña, also from my hometown, who preyed on drug-addicted women and extorted them for sex for years without consequence. Says one of his victims: Magaña came to her "infuriated" that she had complained, demanded more oral sex, ripped off her pants, "touched my genitals with his gun," and said, "If you tell anyone anything about me, I'll blow you up from the inside out," she alleged.

And without internet outrage and viral coverage we would not know the names of FIFTY-TWO unarmed Black men who were killed by police officers. The list includes acquitted insurance underwriter and neighborhood watch volunteer George Zimmerman.

The Thin Blue Line adherents do not have to stop respecting good police. But they must acknowledge that Law Enforcement is not a singular monolith. Police brutality is not universal. Not all cops abuse the badge but not all cops are heroes. Some of them aren't even good. They're actually criminals. And we need to acknowledge the complexity of a monolith composed of individuals. Cops are people. For better and worse.

So to my growing list of white privileges I didn't realize I was enjoying, I add the freedom to not fear the police, the opportunity to respect them, the privilege to run right toward them if I need help, and to know for certain that they will.

And to my gratitude for law enforcement I add outrage for those who not only are not protected by the police but are targeted and violated.

> *"While BLM tries to raise awareness of the segregation and racial exclusion that blacks have faced throughout history, the movement is now trying to enforce the same exclusion on whites."*

# Black Lives Matter Practices the Same Exclusionary Tactics It Professes to Oppose

*Sapna Rampersaud*

*In the following viewpoint, Sapna Rampersaud cites an interview with Lisa Durden on Fox News to suggest that the Black Lives Matter movement is racist. When the BLM Movement excluded non-blacks from a Memorial Day celebration, Durden argued on Fox News that such a decision was fine and that whites were only hurt by this because their "white privilege card" did not allow them access to the celebration. Rampersaud argues that with this decision Black Lives Matter is practicing the same type of exclusionary tactics that they have attributed to whites. Sapna Rampersaud is an intern at* National Review *and studies government, history, and French at Harvard University.*

"The Ideological Problem with Black Lives Matter," by Sapna Rampersaud, National Review, July 6, 2017. Reprinted by permission.

As you read, consider the following questions:

1. Why is it notable that the interview with Durden appeared on Fox news?
2. How could Durden's comments set back the Black Lives Matter movement?
3. How is Sapna Rampersaud's own ethnicity a factor in how she understands this controversy?

The Black Lives Matter movement (BLM), whose mission is to affirm "Black folks' contributions to this society, our humanity, and our resilience in the face of deadly oppression," has a flawed ideology of reparatory racial exclusion that is clearly illustrated in Lisa Durden's interview on Fox News.

Earlier this month, Durden, a professor of media and effective speech at a New Jersey community college, made a televised appearance on *Tucker Carlson Tonight,* where she defended BLM's decision to preclude people who do not identify as black from attending a Memorial Day celebration organized by the movement. Carlson began the interview by reading an excerpt from a statement disseminated by BLM regarding the controversy:

> Being intentional about being around Black People is an act of resistance. This is an exclusively Black Space so if you do not identify as Black and want to come because you love Black People, please respect the space and do not come.

"I'm confused by that," the host followed up, "because I thought the whole point of Black Lives Matter ... would be to speak out against singling people out on the basis of their race and punishing them for that, because you can't control what your race is, and yet they seem to be doing that. Explain that to me."

"What I say to that is boo hoo hoo," Durden shot back. "You white people are angry because you couldn't use your white-privilege card to get invited to the Black Lives Matter's all-black Memorial Day celebration."

## African Americans Benefit from American Privilege

My fellow Americans, the game has been rigged in our favor. This repressive system has been established solely for the purpose of expediting the development of the Western world and is being maintained for our benefit. You, being born in America, inherit a birthright that affords you opportunities that many others could only dream of. The term "American Dream" didn't just pop out of thin air. It derived from very real, very tangible, very measurable discrepancies between life in the West and life around the rest of the world.

As people born into this imbalance, we have two obligations. The first being to recognize the imbalance, and the second being to address how we actively contribute to it. When we deny the existence of this imbalance altogether, we not only justify our privilege but maintain the system that would allow us to continue to benefit from it, making us the oppressors we loathe. Make no mistake, accepting privilege is a painful experience. To accept that you too have played a part in the oppression of others, even as you have cried out against oppression, is an unnerving, guilt-ridden experience.

While BLM tries to raise awareness of the segregation and racial exclusion that blacks have faced throughout history, Durden's comment suggests that the movement is now trying to enforce the same exclusion on whites. The Memorial Day event may have excluded people of other races in order to collectivize blacks and give them a "voice," but this voice is a racist, rather than reasonable, one.

Durden went on to argue that it's okay to exclude white people from Memorial Day celebrations because "we have gay-pride parades, we have Puerto Rican Day parades, we have all kinds of parades and days that honor individuals. We have Mother's Day, we have Father's Day, so on Mother's Day just take your momma out, not your daddy out." Last time I checked, though, straight people could attend gay-pride parades, non–Puerto Ricans could

Uncovering the hidden relationships of privilege means there's no denying it and there's no avoiding it. This is a particularly difficult revelation for American born Black people, who understandably struggle with being both a party to the oppressed and a party to the oppressors. Grappling with the idea that one can be complicit in the oppression of others while still fighting for their own liberation. But contrary to popular belief, we do not live on a secluded island and after almost 500 years in this country, we are as American as they come. Our actions affect the rest of the globe just as much as the actions of our fellow Americans. Neither our complexions nor our oppression make us exempt. After all, we know that there is no privilege without oppression and we know this firsthand.

The time to begin recognizing our place in the world as global citizens is now, not when the rest of the world finally crumbles under our weight. The bad news is it's gonna take a hell of a lot of work on our end. The good news is everyone benefits in the end, including your privileged ass.

"Black Americans, It's Time We Recognize Our Privilege. Our American Privilege." by Arah Iloabugichukwu, Arah the Quill, March 16, 2018. http://www.arahthequill.com/its-time-for-black-americans-to-recognize-their-privilege-american-privilege/

attend Puerto Rican Day parades, fathers could be celebrated on Mother's Day, and mothers could be celebrated on Father's Day.

Durden's comments, as misguided as I think they are, are clearly a response to the years of oppression that black people have experienced in America. But this is the wrong way to rectify the shameful treatment of African Americans throughout our nation's history and the sad legacy it has left. If we collectively discourage, rather than encourage, racial discrimination, the systemic disadvantages that blacks continue to face will wither away. Durden and her ilk, by choosing the opposite path, can only set back the cause of racial progress.

Carlson, to his credit, pointed out as much, calling Durden "hostile," "separatist," and an "apologist" for the BLM movement in their interview, before summing up her stance quite neatly: "I don't care [about] your opinions, I don't care [about] your views, your life experience, your intentions. All I care about is the way you look, something that you can't control, and on that basis alone I'm judging you and I'm hostile to you."

As someone of color whose great-grandparents were brought over to Guyana from India and forced into indentured servitude by the British, I am appalled that people with similar histories (and even those without them) in this generation think it's a good idea to return to those days of exclusion and segregation. I've never felt that, because I was the only non-white person in a class, program, friend group, or job, that I was any less or any different, let alone that it would be wise or desirable to exclude those of other races so I could have a "day to myself" that enhanced my "voice." I fully understand the impulse, of course, given the historic oppression that African Americans have suffered. But when BLM actively decides to promote the same kind of oppression in reverse, it is both counter-productive and disgusting.

> *"This 'color-blind racism' is as dangerous as, if not more dangerous than, the overt racism during Jim Crow. It is for the most part invisible and easily overlooked in public discussions on social issues and therefore very effectively perpetuates racial inequality."*

# "Color-Blindness" Is a Privilege Available Only to White Americans

*Meghan L. Mills*

*In the following viewpoint, Meghan L. Mills argues that Americans' insistence on not seeing color—or their assertions that they are living in a post-racial society—actually do more harm than good. While perhaps well-intentioned, denying the differences between whites and people of color is a privilege afforded only to white people. People of color are reminded on a daily basis that race matters, and they don't have the advantage of turning a blind eye to it. The author contends that admitting this is the first step toward meaningful discourse when it comes to race relations in the United States. Meghan L. Mills is assistant professor of Sociology at Birmingham-Southern College.*

As you read, consider the following questions:

1. What is color-blind racism, according to the viewpoint?
2. Why did the author's students refuse to discuss race on a meaningful level?
3. What does it mean to apply a "sociological imagination," according to the viewpoint?

F ollowing the recent events featured in the media such as the riots in Baltimore that came after the fatal shooting of Freddie Gray, Rachel Dolezal stepping down as the Spokane Washington NAACP president, and the tragic shootings in Charleston, South Carolina, public discussions have primarily focused on issues surrounding individual responsibility and mental illness.

I read these conversations with disappointment and frustration. The dominant approach to understanding racial inequality in the US today is "color-blind racism." This is the belief that racial inequality can be attributed only to issues considered to be "race-neutral". In other words, because racial discrimination is now illegal, everyone is born with an equal opportunity to achieve the "American Dream," no matter their race.

In comparison to the overt and legal racism prior to the Civil Rights movement, this "new" transformed type of racism is seemingly invisible, making meaningful societal discussions near impossible, and in turn perpetuating racial inequality, which then expresses itself, as we have seen, in these recent incidents.

## Conversations with Students

What about classrooms? Are adequate conversations around race taking place in that space? And how can scholars shape some of the discussions?

A clear example of "color-blind racism" unexpectedly arose my first year as an assistant professor of sociology at Birmingham-Southern College (BSC) in Birmingham, Alabama.

Being a "Yankee," I was warned in advance that my students at BSC would be more politically and socially conservative than what I was used to (coming from the University of New Hampshire).

However, midway into my first semester, I found that the majority of my students were able to critically engage in potentially controversial topics such as LGBT rights, health care reform and the legalization of marijuana. We also discussed the class inequality between them as middle- or upper-class students living within the gated "hilltop" campus and the surrounding lower social class neighborhood immediately outside of the campus gates.

The real challenge arose when it came to discussing race in the classroom.

I struggled to get my students to address the "elephant in the room"—that the majority of the surrounding lower social class neighborhood comprised racial minorities, whereas the majority of my students and BSC professors, including myself, benefited from "white privilege," the often unacknowledged advantages with which whites are born, based solely on the color of their skin.

## Challenges of Talking About Race

I had incorrectly assumed that teaching in Birmingham, Alabama, with its rich social and cultural history of the Civil Rights movement and racial heterogeneity, would make discussing racial inequality one of the most engaging and meaningful discussions in the course.

My students refused to discuss race beyond a superficial level.

I found the majority of my students, primarily from the South, have been "socialized" to not discuss race because "race doesn't matter" and we are (or should be) a "color-blind" society.

This was illustrated by student responses such as "there is only one race: human" and "only racists see race" when asked in class whether race still matters. The responses were consistently given by students across my four classes.

Conversations with several of my faculty colleagues across disciplines also revealed that this was a common theme.

What I learned was that in order to get students to more effectively discuss issues of race, I needed to first address one of the most dangerous social myths perpetuating racial inequality in today's society—that we are a "color-blind" society.

## How to Teach Race

I have modified my lesson on race to begin, not end, with a discussion of "color-blind racism." What I have found to be most critical to this discussion is challenging my students to apply their "sociological imaginations," which can enable them to look at underlying social issues behind some recent news events.

As good sociologists-in-training, my students are asked to consider the larger social structural concerns (eg, poverty, institutional racism, the criminal justice system) instead of focusing on individuals (eg, Baltimore police officers, Rachael Dolezal, Dylann Roof).

My experiences in the classroom are by no means an isolated incident. Research consistently indicates this "color-blind" ideology permeates education, politics, the criminal justice system, the media, etc.

This "color-blind racism" is as dangerous as, if not more dangerous than, the overt racism during Jim Crow. It is for the most part invisible and easily overlooked in public discussions on social issues and therefore very effectively perpetuates racial inequality.

If the majority of my college students believe it is wrong to even "see" race, how can they be expected to meaningfully discuss larger issues of institutional racism and inequality? How can we as a society expect more meaningful social discussions and solutions?

As scholars, we need to emphasize to our students that race is a real thing, with real consequences. As long as we as a society continue avoiding "seeing" or meaningfully discussing race, we will continue to have Baltimore riots and Charleston shootings.

> *"Dolezal committed the ultimate white privilege act: she donned blackface when it was convenient for her with the escape hatch wide open to return to her Whiteness whenever she so chose to. No surgical altering is done. Bronzer off, Whiteness on."*

# "Real" Black People Don't Have the Option to Turn Off Their Color

Jennifer Floyd

*In the following viewpoint Jennifer Floyd argues that we cannot decide to be a certain race when it's convenient or when we feel like it. The author reacts to the case of Rachel Dolezal, a white woman who claimed to be African American. As the author contends, black people in America do not have the luxury of living as the race they "feel" like (as Dolezal claimed in identifying as an African American). Unfortunately, most black people cannot hide their race and must be subject to disparities in treatment and privilege simply because of the way they look. Jennifer Floyd is a music and culture writer based in San Antonio, Texas.*

"Rant & Rave: No, Rachel Dolezal Is Not Black & Never Will Be No Matter How Much She 'Feels It,'" by Jennifer Floyd, Jen on the Rocks, http://www.jenontherocks.com/2015/06/rant-rave-no-rachel-dolezal-is-not.html. Licensed under CC BY 4.0 International.

As you read, consider the following questions:

1. What did Rachel Dolezal do that made her part of the national conversation?
2. Why does the author reject comparisons between Dolezal and Caitlyn Jenner?
3. Why isn't Dolezal's action the same as "passing," according to the viewpoint?

M ichael Jackson sang, "It doesn't matter if you're Black or White", but somewhere down the line Rachel Dolezal decided that being Black was all that she wanted to be. The prominent Washington civil rights leader and NAACP president has claimed for 17 years that she is a "sista," but her parents have recently come out to say the opposite, unveiling via photos that Dolezal is actually a White woman who is passing herself off as a Black woman.

Oh, dear …

Speaking to the Spokane-Spokesman Review, Dolezal's mother claimed that her 37-year-old daughter started to "disguise herself" after her family adopted four African-American children. Dolezal continued to assimilate into African-American culture after she applied and gained an art scholarship to Howard University, winding up becoming a adjunct professor of Africana studies at Eastern Washington University.

Dolezal's lasagna of lies caved in when she reported nine alleged hate crimes over the course of 10 years to the authorities and an investigation was conducted to bring legitimacy to her claims. Dolezal had claimed she received hate mail in her NAACP post office box, but it was discovered that the letters weren't from outside sources, but rather, sent from Dolezal's own box.

Dolezal's jig was thoroughly up when a journalist investigating the claims pressed her about her racial background, presenting her with a photo of her standing next to an older African-American man, whom Dolezal had persistently claimed to be her biological father. As the journalist cleanly asked: "Are you African-American?," Dolezal and her Barbara Streisand *A Star Is Born* wig retched in response: "I don't understand the question."

Naturally, when this story broke, the Internet had a field day, and Twitter had the spit up and ready to roast.

But as the smoke and laughter clears, I have to now fix my side-eye steady, especially at the people who are donning capes to save Dolezal's reputation, calling her charade a "bold" and "courageous" move that transcends how we as a society think about race and culture and the occupying of it. Caitlyn Jenner's name is being tossed around to justify Dolezal and her choice to "choose" to be a particular race, because if you can choose and alter your gender like Jenner and countless other transgender individuals, why not choose and alter you race?

I have no idea why this thought is even being entertained.

For the most part it's a nice little deflection as it excuses Dolezal's bold act of culture appropriation in favor of being too damn politically correct, and too damn simple. None of what Dolezal did has pushed any sort of revolutionary idea about identity or constructed a "trans-racial" narrative adjacent to transgenderism. Trans-racialism isn't about the switching of races, it's about the social and cultural blending of adopted families. Dolezal committed the ultimate white privilege act: she donned blackface when it was convenient for her with the escape hatch wide open to return to her Whiteness whenever she so chose to. No surgical altering is done. Bronzer off, Whiteness on.

To be an ally, to be "down for the cause," you do not disrespect the culture and the people within the culture by misrepresenting who you are and where you're coming from. That just defeats the purpose. I mean, if you can't advocate for people without the need to deceive, how truly genuine is your concern? Dolezal could've utilized her privilege for some good, there was nothing wrong with her joining the NAACP as a white woman, and being involved in Black causes. Nobody would've batted eyes or groused about it. Dolezel, instead, let her self-entitlement show as she costumed herself in sister girl stereotypes, and used Black people as props, wedging, specifically Black women out of the conversation and squatted in the space, not for progress, but for her own personal, financial, and professional fulfillment, and it makes her, the NAACP, and everyone who bought it and supported it look foolish.

Dolezal's act isn't in the same historical context of light-skinned Black people and bi-racials passing as White to escape racism and to gain social opportunities affronted to Whites, as when these individuals did the switcheroo and were revealed of their true identities they were met with serious offenses, sometimes criminal and other times death. Dolezal didn't get sucked down into "quicksand," she wasn't playing in 'imitation of life' game, she presented a *Soul Man* con, misguided individuals who believed she was helping them, and made a deceptive mockery off of Black women's plights and thought the whole charade was cute.

If you peek at her social media pages (now all turned private), Dolezal was taking cultural appropriation to an insane hashtag and Perpetua filtered level, and as more layers are unveiled, you have to marvel at her diligence to keep up with such a farce.

As a mellow yellow, florescent beige sista I feel pressed like an acrylic nail over how for seventeen years Dolezal upheld this delusion, that nobody questioned her Blackness when mines has continuously been brought to doubt. For all the times I've been told I wasn't "Black enough" due to my light skin and grade of hair, Dolezal glided past these inquires, and to call it mentally screwy doesn't even begin to sum it up, especially since Dolezal expressed that she would take a DNA test after she insisted to an interviewer she was African-American. The catch is, as Vox.com states, there isn't a DNA test for African-American identity as race is a social construct—not a biological one.

It's phenomenal being a Black woman, I know, we've got flow and a presence that can't be denied, so I can see why Rachael Dolezal felt the need to co-opt, but to all those who believe this 'vanilla child' should be considered Black strictly because she 'feels' so, need to put down your New Black City pamphlets and look at the real world. Dolezal can don Jane Child braids, slow wine her speech, and cake on the Fashion Fair pressed powder, but in a physical and social context she will never be a African-American, never be a Black woman. She can "feel it" all she wants, but being a Black person in America isn't something you wake up and decide to be and then peel off like a facial peel at the end of the day. It's just not that simple.

Dolezal is just another culture vulture enacting their privilege to push us all back hundreds of years. She isn't "down for the cause" no matter what motivated her to do what she did, respect went out the window when she claimed to be something she wasn't and professionally benefited off of it. Laugh at her, yes, feel a pinch of pity for her, maybe, but don't try to justify what truly isn't there, because it's all smoke, weaves, and bronzer—and none of that stuff makes you exclusively Black last I checked.

# Periodical and Internet Sources Bibliography

*The following articles have been selected to supplement the diverse views presented in this chapter.*

Charlotte Allen, "Beyond the Pale." *Weekly Standard.* May 27, 2013. https://www.weeklystandard.com/charlotte-allen/beyond-the-pale-724717

Alex Blasdel, "Is white America ready to confront its racism? Philosopher George Yancy says we need a 'crisis.'" Apr. 24, 2018. https://www.theguardian.com/world/2018/apr/24/george-yancy-dear-white-america-philosopher-confront-racism

Joseph Cesario, "A new look at racial disparities in police use of deadly force." July 31, 2018. https://theconversation.com/a-new-look-at-racial-disparities-in-police-use-of-deadly-force-98681

Victor Davis Hanson, "The White-Privilege Tedium," *National Review.* October 23, 2018. https://www.nationalreview.com/2018/10/white-privilege-debate-elizabeth-warren/

Kut Staff, "It's Up To White People To Discuss And Confront Racism, Minister Says." Kut. Apr. 6, 2018. https://www.kut.org/post/its-white-people-discuss-and-confront-racism-minister-says

German Lopez, "Study: anti-black hiring discrimination is as prevalent today as it was in 1989." Vox. Sept. 18, 2017. https://www.vox.com/identities/2017/9/18/16307782/study-racism-jobs

John Meinhold, "My Turn: The myth of white privilege in America." *Concord Monitor.* Dec. 14, 2017. https://www.concordmonitor.com/The-myth-of-white-privilege-13988254

Mark Oppenheimer, "Some Evangelicals Struggle With Black Lives Matter Movement." *New York Times.* Jan. 22, 2016. https://www.nytimes.com/2016/01/23/us/some-evangelicals-struggle-with-black-lives-matter-movement.html?_r=0

Erik Ortiz. "'Wow, I'm racist': In time of viral encounters, 'white spaces' are used to confront biases." Dec. 24, 2018. https://www.nbcnews.com/news/us-news/wow-i-m-racist-time-viral-encounters-white-spaces-are-n947311

Max J. Romano, "White Privilege in a White Coat: How Racism Shaped my Medical Education." *Annals of Family Medicine. May/*

*June 2018 vol. 16 no. 3 261-263*. http://www.annfammed.org/content/16/3/261.full

"White privilege does not exist." Hotep Nation. Accessed May 6, 2019. https://www.hotepnation.com/white-privilege-not-exist/

Joanna Williams, "No, I Won't Check My Privilege." *American Conservative*. May 25, 2018. https://www.theamericanconservative.com/articles/no-i-wont-check-my-privilege/

Mike Wilner. "Acknowledging Privilege to Tackle Inequality." Dec. 17, 2014. https://medium.com/@mwil20/acknowledging-privilege-to-tackle-inequality-65b1fd00b52a

Matthew Yglesias, "The Great Awokening." Vox. Apr. 1, 2019. https://www.vox.com/2019/3/22/18259865/great-awokening-white-liberals-race-polling-trump-2020

Laura Youngkin, "How I Learned to See My White Privilege as a Responsibility." Yellow Co. April 20, 2018. https://yellowco.co/blog/2018/04/20/learned-see-white-privilege-responsibility/

OPPOSING
VIEWPOINTS®
SERIES

CHAPTER 3

# How Does Male Privilege Affect Women?

# Chapter Preface

In discussions of male privilege and feminism, it is a commonplace to cite the "gender pay gap," which refers to the difference in salary that women in the workplace are paid versus what men earn. This disparity has been calculated as being 78 percent. That is, women take in 78 percent of what their male peers earn. Each year various feminist organizations recognize Equal Pay Day, the symbolic date on which women finally earn as much as men did the previous year. In 2019, Equal Pay Day occurred on April 2. In other words, women must work 92 days into the next year (or 457 days in total) to earn what men brought in during the previous 365 days. To many, this incongruity is one prominent example of male privilege.

Are women's lives impeded by a societally approved, ingrained hierarchy that privileges males? The answer depends on whom you ask. Conservatives are likely to argue that there is little-to-no wage pay gap when we strip out factors such as women who choose, voluntarily, to work part time; or that most women gain less experience or have fewer years on the job due to child care leaves of absence; or that women have traditionally chosen occupations that offer less remuneration. Carrie Lucas, writing for the conservative *National Review*, notes the progress women have made in narrowing the wage gap over the years, and discredits the feminist narrative of a demeaning wage gap: "The public should reject the tired logic of the feminist movement that seems intent on denying that women ever make any progress and convincing the next generation of women that America is overwhelmingly sexist and they are doomed to being consistently shortchanged," she contends.

Writing for the liberal *Huffington Post*, Emily Peck begs to differ: "The gender wage gap is actually worse than you think," she asserts, "with women earning slightly less than half of what men make over the long term, according to a report released [on November 26, 2018] by the Institute for Women's Policy Research."

So it goes for most topics when it comes to male privilege and all of its repercussions, including the glass ceiling, rape culture, sexual harassment, and the #MeToo movement. Columnists on the left will say that although progress is being made, there is still a long way to go. Those on the right will argue that progress is being made, and society is very near to solving these issues.

The truth probably lies somewhere in the middle.

An impediment to change is the attitude of men themselves. As a privileged group, they do not notice their status, which many feminists say is unearned, any more than a fish notices it is swimming in water. As Peggy McInstosh writes, "Only rarely will a man go beyond acknowledging that women are disadvantaged to acknowledging that men have unearned advantage, or that unearned privilege has not been good for men's development as human beings, or for society's development, or that privilege systems might ever be challenged and changed."

As a whole, men are unlikely to cede their privilege system anytime soon, especially when many consider the entire concept of male privilege to be a feminist fantasy. Writing in the British *Spectator*, Brendan O'Neill cites polls that show young men are the most derided group in England, viewed as "drunken, promiscuous, prone to drug-taking, work-shy and impolite." Moreover, he says, young women now earn more than young men in the 22-29 age group: over £1100 (about $1400).

And here is the entry on male privilege in the crowd-sourced Urban Dictionary:

> A myth fabricated and spread by feminists, primarily liberal and progressive ones, to use as the excuse for why women are not dominating every aspect of life including politics, STEM, and other jobs. This conspiracy theory automatically assumes all men are not only successful as a whole, but that they have only earned what they have because of their gender. To believe

in the existence of male privilege one must also believe that the world is controlled by the patriarchy.

Those "liberals and progressives" would likely argue that both O'Neill and the Urban Dictionary entry entirely miss the point: that by virtue of their sex, men do come into this world with certain unearned advantages that are usually denied to women. Male privilege does not mean that every male has used this status effectively enough to gain a better place in society or achieve success. It only means that men have an inherent societal advantage.

But their detractors would probably come back at them twice as hard. Perhaps the feminists are correct on this point: they do have a long way to go to alter such attitudes.

> *"Kimmel's comedic, tactically performed talk paired with the accusations of harassment and sexism is indicative of performative allyship, where one publicly advocates for social justice principles, and often profits off of it, but does not behave according to those principles in their day-to-day life."*

# Gender Equality Leaders Must Be Held Accountable

*Lindsey Jones-Renaud*

*In the following viewpoint, Lindsey Jones-Renaud discusses the case of Michael Kimmel, an expert on gender equality who has been accused of sexual harassment. She attended a TED Talk where Kimmel made a sexual joke. A globally recognized expert had the privilege to get away with such a tactic, where most others could not. But the hypocrisy of Kimmel's situation suggest to Jones-Renaud that more female experts need to lead the work of achieving gender equality, not males. Those who do lead must be held accountable. Lindsey Jones-Renaud is a project manager, gender equality expert, and community advocate in Washington, DC, who writes about gender, whiteness, philanthropy, and development.*

"Accountability and Men's Leadership in Gender Equality", by Lindsey Jones-Renaud (Founder and Principal Consultant of Cynara Development Services), Medium.com, August 23, 2018. Reprinted by permission.

As you read, consider the following questions:

1. Why was Jones-Renauld uncomfortable during Kimmel's TED Talk?
2. What lessons can be taken from Kimmel's situation?
3. How can gender equality leaders be held accountable?

Michael Kimmel, professor of sociology at Stoney Brook University in New York and globally recognized expert on engaging men and boys for gender equality, was part of a training I gave a few months ago. He was not there in person, but I used a quote and picture of him to illustrate how power and privilege are at the root of all identity-based violence, including sexual harassment. His quote, "privilege is invisible to those who have it," is painfully true as he has become one of the latest public figures to be accused of harassment, sexism, and misogyny in the age of #MeToo and #AidToo.

Around the same time that I conducted that training, I was invited to a talk Kimmel gave at an agency in Washington, D.C., about why gender equality is a win-win for everyone. His presentation was reminiscent of his 2015 TEDtalk; he walked confidently around the stage as he spoke in front of a large crowd of people across the gender spectrum, telling jokes and offering tweetable, witty statements about gender equality such as "without confronting men's sense of entitlements, we can't achieve gender equality."

Toward the end of his talk, he shared a series of business cases for why men should care about gender equality. Making a business case for gender equality is a common vernacular in the philanthropic business and international development sectors. I cannot remember all the cases Kimmel made for gender equality, but I do remember that he presented them using comedic public speaking techniques, building up each one after the other as if he was approaching a punchline. And he was. I cannot remember the exact words, but essentially his punchline was this: *if none of the other business cases don't convince you to support gender equality, consider the fact that husbands and wives who share housework and childcare have more sex than couples who don't.*

While his statement is backed by research, his emphasis on this point as being the ultimate case for men to support gender equality played into heteronormative, gender stereotypes about men as sex-crazed creatures juxtaposed against women's laughable disinterest in sex. It reflected society's tendency to remove women of their sexual agency by placing the source of any presumed disinterest in sex with housework and childrearing instead of sexuality or pleasure. Further, there was no space in this business case for gender equality that includes genderqueer and non-binary genders. It excludes uncoupled people, women who are partnered with women, and men who are partnered with men.

I remember being surprised that he essentially joked about sex at workplace event. In the midst of #MeToo and #AidToo movements, organizations are hastily training employees in how not to harass their colleagues and sexual jokes is an obvious example of what not to do. I also remember most of the people in the room were laughing, indicating they were enjoying his talk. I was a guest in the space and it was not my workplace. I felt lucky to be there and listen to someone whose work I admired. I observed how much everyone seemed to enjoy his talk and so I told others that I did too. I told myself that surely, he had systems of accountability in place, such as advisors of various genders who give him honest feedback on his presentations and interpretations of research.

I wonder how many people were uncomfortable like I was but also remained quiet about it. Self-doubt and the fear of retaliation— in this case, being told I did not appreciate humor—is a powerful enabler of harassment and injustice. Kimmel's power and privilege as an internationally recognized scholar and speaker enabled him to tell a joke that could get other people fired and kept me from speaking up. This was not visible to me at the time, though I certainly felt it and responded to those feelings. While Kimmel was correct that privilege is often invisible to those who have it, it is especially powerful when it is also invisible to those who do not. It keeps us from speaking up.

## What This Means for Engaging Men in Gender Equality

In light of the claims of sexual harassment and sexism, Kimmel resigned from the board of Promundo, a leading international organization working to engage men and boys in gender justice. A simple Google search shows how the international philanthropy and development sector is ripe with discussion about "engaging men" to advance gender equality, which has become more popular in recent years in part due to the #HeforShe campaign.

These initiatives are all important. But the claims against Michael Kimmel highlight two important things that are missing in the way the sector talks about engaging men and boys in gender equality, and for the social inclusion space at large.

## ONE: We Must Make the Space and Provide Resources for Women, Girls, and Non-Binary Experts to Lead This Work

Kimmel's comedic, tactically performed talk paired with the accusations of harassment and sexism is indicative of performative allyship, where one publicly advocates for social justice principles, and often profits off of it, but does not behave according to those principles in their day-to-day life. Performative allyship is not uncommon in the gender equality space, and it is therefore no surprise that many women are suspicious of men who self-identify as leaders for gender equality.

We need to be wary of performative allyship in the philanthropy and development sectors. We must be amplifying the voices of women, girls, and non-binary people—especially those in the countries where international development is working—and learning from them about how to engage men and boys. This does not mean that men and boys cannot contribute, but there is much to learn from the work women, girls, and non-binary folks are doing every day to shift gender norms and advocate for their rights. As Srilatha Batliwala of the Association for Women's Rights in Development pointed out in 2014, grassroots women's organizations have always worked with men and boys:

> ... in the South Asian context that I know best, most organizations that work to empower women and tackle gender inequality in communities—whether rural or urban; poor, working class, or middle class—have ALWAYS had to work with men and boys, in one way or another. Indeed, one could not mobilize or build women's collective power while ignoring the men in those women's lives ... we didn't see it as a distinct strategic component, but an organic part of our organizing.

Global north institutions must be careful not to appropriate what they learn from those most directly affected, but instead make the space and provide the resources to amplify their voices and statuses as leaders in the sector. Philanthropic organizations are great at talking about how they empower women and girls, but few are able or willing to disclose the proportion of money they distribute to women-led institutions in the global south, not to mention institutions led by people with non-binary gender identities.

## TWO: To Successfully Engage Men in Gender Equality Work, We Must Talk About Accountability

We can't talk about engaging men and boys without talking about power and accountability. I agree that gender equality is not a zero-sum game; it will benefit everyone. However, inequality is ultimately about an imbalance of power. Therefore, to get to gender equality, men—and to some extent, boys—will have to surrender some of the power and privilege that comes with being male. We need systems of accountability, such as those put forth by the Athena Network and the MenEngage Alliance, to ensure that that this is actually happening. Without accountability, self-identified allies like Michael Kimmel are able to thrive, reproducing unjust power structures, perpetuating gender stereotypes, and causing harm to the women, girls, and gender non-conforming folks they are intending to help.

Humanitarian aid and development organizations rarely take accountability seriously. Over 120 CEOs of leading international humanitarian and development organizations signed a pledge on preventing sexual abuse, harassment, and exploitation. Most of these CEOs are white people and male. Yet there is only one mention of accountability, and it is only with regards to specific incidents of sexual abuse. The pledge, which was organized by the network InterAction, does not say anything about how they will be held accountable to these commitments.

## These Lessons Apply to All Forms of Power and Privilege

The lack of accountability systems and practices of making space for underrepresented groups is not limited to male engagement in gender equality spaces. It also applies to other inequalities: racial, global, gender identity, sexual orientation, ability, and so on. It is too easy for women like me—white women from countries in the global north—to criticize men like Michael Kimmel but ignore our own responsibility to make spaces for women of color, women from the global south, people with disabilities, transgender people, and people of other marginalized groups, to drive philanthropy and development. As much as women deserve ways to hold male allies of gender equality accountable, we also have the responsibility to hold ourselves accountable in the fight for social justice and inclusion.

In fact, these lessons apply to anyone in a position of power. As Tarana Burke, who founded the #MeToo movement, said in response to men who have come forward with stories of harassment by women in powerful positions:

> It will continue to be jarring when we hear the names of some of our [favorite people] connected to sexual violence unless we shift from talking about individuals and begin to talk about

## I HATE TO BREAK IT TO FEMINISTS, BUT "WHITE MALE PRIVILEGE" IS A MYTH

How's this for dark irony: throughout 2015, 'white male privilege' was the buzzphrase on every rad tweeter and liberal hack's lips, as they fumed against the easy, pampered lives allegedly enjoyed by human beings who had the fortune to be born with a penis and pale skin. Railing against 'white men' and their cushy existences has become the stock-in-trade of many feminists.

Yet towards the end of 2015 it was revealed that there's a social group in Britain more derided and less successful than pretty much every other social group. Guess who? Yep, young white men. Especially young working-class white men. A large sector of the group that the new identity-politics mob loves to ridicule for sailing through life unmolested and unchallenged is actually having a rough time.

Consider this: 18-year-old women are 35 percent more likely to attend university than 18-year-old men; and where 37 percent of black school-leavers go to university, only 28 percent of white school-leavers do. These stats were unveiled by UCAS in December, leading its chief executive to wonder if it isn't time to initiate 'outreach' projects designed to get more white blokes into college.

power. Sexual violence is about power and privilege. That doesn't change if the perpetrator is your favorite actress, activist or professor of any gender. And we won't shift the culture unless we get serious about shifting these false narratives.

## An Alternative Model for Michael Kimmel

I cannot speak to the allegations against Kimmel and how he could repair the harm experienced by those individuals. However, when it comes to the speaking engagement I witnessed, here are a few steps he could have taken that may have enabled it to turn out differently:

- Be transparent about his systems of accountability, such as by describing it in a section on his website. Perhaps all

Also in December, a YouGov analysis of 48 surveys of public attitudes found that young white men are viewed as 'the worst ethnic, gender [and] age group'. They are 'the most derided ethnic group in Britain'. YouGov's number-crunchers confessed to being surprised by 'the lousy reputation of young white men', who are seen as drunken, promiscuous, prone to drug-taking, work-shy and impolite (even as other surveys reveal that today's yoof actually drink less and do fewer drugs than earlier generations did).

What's more, young women now earn more than young men: £1,111 a year more, to be precise. Between the ages of 22 and 29, women in general—covering all races—out-earn guys; by the time women hit their thirties, however, their pay falls below men's. Those young, opinionated new media feminists who get handsome advances to write books spluttering about 'white male privilege' are far more privileged than many of the white males they splutter about—especially the ones who empty their bins or sweep their roads. It's almost Orwellian in its topsy-turviness—the most well-connected, middle-class women denouncing the alleged privileges of some of the most derided people in society.

"I hate to break it to feminists, but 'white male privilege' is a myth," by Brendan O'Neill, The Spectator, January 5, 2016.

organizations who claim to have a social impact should do this, myself included.

- Use his speaking engagements as an opportunity to amplify the voices of people of diverse genders and identities, whether by having co-speakers, including them in video clips, or featuring their quotes during his presentation.
- Explicitly talk about accountability during his presentation as being a critical component of men's roles in promoting gender equality.
- Hire an advisory committee made up of people from diverse genders and identities who can provide regular and honest feedback.

These are all ways of sharing and redistributing the power that comes with his privilege, reputation, and scholarly position. Yes, privilege is often invisible to those who have it; but the solution is not just making privilege more visible, it is finding ways to redress the disproportionate power that comes with it.

> "It is obviously not the case that this 'malestream' perspective is one simply shared by all men, and no women. The 'male eye' view is one organised around gender stereotypes that subordinate women, the 'second sex,' in a way that benefits a determinate class of men."

# The Language of "Privilege" Is Inadequate

### Richard Seymour

*In the following viewpoint Richard Seymour argues that he disagrees with the language of privilege, not because it doesn't make a good point, but because it can be unhelpfully moralistic. Seymour speaks instead of the "male eye" with regard to men's advantages in society. This is the lens through which not all but many men view the world and rationalize the power men have over women. Even though it would seem that men benefit from such a system, it actually works against everyone. Richard Seymour is a political activist who blogs at Lenin's Tomb. He is the author of* Against Austerity: How We Can Fix the Crisis They Made.

"On 'Male Privilege,'" by Richard Seymour, Guardian News and Media Limited. February 21, 2013. Reprinted by permission.

As you read, consider the following questions:

1. How do the "white eye" and the "male eye" reinforce patterns of dominance, according to the author?
2. How does so-called "rape culture" traffic in denial?
3. What are examples of how the repercussions of the male eye weaken society as a whole?

I profoundly disagree with the language of "privilege". The discourse seems inadequate to the complex realities of racial, gender, and national inequalities for example. It also tends, in concrete politics, toward an unhelpfully moralistic language— checking your privilege, and so on. However, I don't think one should be afraid of it. Not just for macho reasons—though it's true that I am quite a big boy now, and can stand to hear things I disagree with. Rather, like many problematic-yet-persistent concepts, it's getting at something real. And when "male privilege" and its effects are raised in this context, to explain how implicitly sexist assumptions can be reproduced without much thought, it does seem to be addressing a real problem (this is not a comment on Owen Jones; I'm speaking generally).

I am reminded of Stuart Hall's discussion of the implicit "white eye" view in the media. It is not that every white person equally shares in this point of view, or is equally responsible for it, or is equally implicated in it. Far from it. This implied perspective arises from complex sets of ideological representations that are largely produced in the ideological state apparatuses by the ruling class and its allies. Naturally, since ideology is a field of struggle and contest, these ideological representations must also incorporate "popular" elements if they are to be effective. But the "white eye" is not the "eye" of an essential "whiteness"; it is the "eye" of a historically produced mode of domination, from which a minority of ruling white men derive most of the benefit.

The "white eye" is not what is seen, moreover. It is outside the frame, but seems to shape everything in it: a present-absent cause, it exerts a gravitational pull around which a discursive field of racist assumptions is organised. The implied perspective, simply because it is implied and never explicated, forms a "common sense" so that those articulating it speak with great assurance. The onus is on those disputing it to disprove its assumptions—to prove that immigrants aren't deviants and leeches, the black families are not dysfunctional sources of crime, that "Islam" is not a particular solvent of values or security menace, etc.

So it might be with "male privilege" referred to in this sense. Adapting Hall, one might speak of "those apparently naturalised representations of events and situations relating to sex and gender, whether 'factual' or 'fictional', which have sexist premisses and propositions inscribed in them as a set of unquestioned assumptions" and which "enable sexist statements to be formulated without ever bringing into awareness the sexist predicates on which the statements are grounded." It is obviously not the case that this "malestream" perspective is one simply shared by all men, and no women. The "male eye" view is one organised around gender stereotypes that subordinate women, the "second sex", in a way that benefits a determinate class of men.

What is called "rape culture", which has been the focus of the recent radicalisation of women's struggles, is but one particularly obnoxious variant of this phenomenon. Take some of the usual tropes: "women ask for it sometimes"; "only bad girls get raped"; "women get raped because they get drunk and show off their bodies"; "women cry rape because they've been jilted, or have something to hide"; "women's bodies, if they genuinely don't want sex, shut down". Underlying these are various fundamental gender binaries: male activity v female passivity; male rationality v female hysteria; male seriousness v female deviousness; and so on.

Notably, these tropes mostly don't explicitly condone rape. Rather I think they can be related to the three categories of denial identified by Stan Cohen: 1) *literal denial*, wherein it is asserted that no such thing happened, and the woman must be a liar, a fantasist or unwell; 2) *interpretive denial*, wherein some of the facts are admitted, but it's suggested that in context it's not as bad as it seems, because the woman was drunk, or drugged, or is likely a prostitute, or was dressed provocatively; and 3) *implicatory denial*, where it's admitted that the facts are as they're said to be, and very bad indeed, but, well, there's nothing that can be done about it anyway, rape is just a part of life, the best thing is for women concerned is to dress down, not stay out late, not drink, etc. Things are much worse overseas, anyway: you're lucky you don't live there. The result of such strategies of denial is to mobilise implicit assumptions about women into a story, as narrated from a "male eye" view, which normalises and naturalises rape, and blunts the force of any challenge to it.

It would be grotesque to say that enabling the perpetuation of rape thereby preserves or protects any "privilege" for men. But clearly the gendered tropes that are pressed into the service of rape culture are bound up with the ostensible compensations of "maleness", this "psychological wage" as Du Bois put it in a different context. Of course, these compensations are not simply "psychological". They are an iteration at the level of ideology of various realities—the wage gap, male household dominance, the orientation of mass culture toward encouraging women to be "man-pleasing", and so on. In the total, longer-term view, all of these realities actually cost men. The wage gap, for example, is part of maintaining a stratified labour system that undermines the bargaining strength and political cohesion of labour, and thus reduces the overall wage claims of both men and women. But social interests are always construed through social representations, and one might say that the implied "male eye" view of a great deal of mass media and academic output provides the appropriate grid through which these compensations can be perceived and lived as a real privilege.

This "psychological wage", which some might still prefer to call "male privilege", is necessary to explain the investment that too many people have in these strategies of denial, which otherwise serve to reinforce a deeply harmful pattern of sexual violence and hypocrisy, a combination of prurience and puritanism that leaves no one better off. Necessary, I should add, but not sufficient.

> "The most effective mentors are
> people with a wealth of professional
> experience, those already in
> leadership positions. More often than
> not, that means they're men."

# Female Empowerment Is Causing a Male Backlash

*Stéphanie Thomson*

*In the following viewpoint, Stéphanie Thomson writes that there is no simple answer to ending workplace gender inequality, but mentoring is a valuable strategy. However, in the wake of the #MeToo movement, male leaders are becoming more hesitant to work with female protégés, for fear that they will be targeted for inappropriate behavior. Thompson offers a range of suggestions about how to overcome this reluctance, but she ultimately believes that, if women are not valued in a particular workplace, they should find another more welcoming company. A global trade expert, Stéphanie Thomson is a writer and former editor at the World Economic Forum.*

As you read, consider the following questions:

1. What has Sylvia Ann Hewlett's research revealed about male executives' attitudes toward mentoring?
2. What is Facebook COO Sheryl Sandberg's attitude toward male executive mentoring?
3. What specific strategies can overcome male reluctance to mentor women protégés?

I f there were a simple way of ending workplace gender inequality, we wouldn't be where we are today—still living in a man's world.

But this lack of progress doesn't mean there aren't tried-and-tested strategies. One of those is pretty simple: mentoring. Researchers have found mentors can help with everything from closing the gender gap in STEM subjects to getting more women into leadership roles.

In fact, for Belle Rose Ragins, a professor at the Lubar School of Business who has been studying workplace diversity for decades, mentoring could be one of the most effective ways of achieving equality at work. "Our research has found that mentoring is one of the main strategies used by women who have made their way to the top," she explains. "Mentoring relationships are the chisels that help women break through the glass ceiling."

The most effective mentors are people with a wealth of professional experience, those already in leadership positions. More often than not, that means they're men. "Male mentors are particularly important, as men typically have more power than women in most organizations," Ragins points out.

There's just one small problem: all too often, men aren't comfortable taking female protégés under their wings. That's the conclusion reached by Sylvia Ann Hewlett, CEO of the Centre for Talent Innovation. "Our research shows that some 64% of senior men avoid solo interactions with junior women because they fear rumours about their motives," she says.

And that was before the #MeToo revolution. What started out as a hashtash used by actresses to highlight sexual abuse in Hollywood quickly spread, exposing male predators in just about every industry. While many male allies saw the movement as an opportunity to listen and better understand how they could help, some men had a different reaction, instead deciding it was safer to limit contact with their female colleagues. Fears of a backlash that would reverse all progress have quickly spread.

These concerns are based on more than just anecdotes from watercooler conversations. According to a survey commissioned by the Lean In initiative, the number of male managers who are uncomfortable mentoring women has tripled since the #MeToo movement first started back in October 2017.

For Facebook COO Sheryl Sandberg, who set up the foundation, these findings are something to worry about. "If men think that the way to address workplace sexual harassment is to avoid one-on-one time with female colleagues—including meetings, coffee breaks and all the interactions that help us work together effectively—it will be a huge setback for women," she wrote in a Facebook post.

But it is possible to turn this moment into positive change. As Ragins notes, these issues existed long before the hashtag; now they're out in the open, we can actually start addressing them rather than acting like they're not there.

"We need to get to the root of this discomfort," she says. "Is it because the male mentor is afraid he may be sexually attracted to his female protégé? Does he fear others will misinterpret their relationship as sexual? Or is he afraid his female protégé may misinterpret his actions as sexual in nature? These questions and issues have always been present in cross-gender mentoring relationships. The #MeToo movement brings them to light and offers the possibility of meaningful dialogue that will address and hopefully ameliorate these concerns."

Are there practices and techniques that might help? Certainly. Formalizing mixed-mentorship programmes is a good place to begin, Hewlett has found. "Companies can squelch whispering campaigns before they get started by designating safe spaces where senior male leaders can publicly get together with female protégés for breakfast, lunch or coffee. By naming a specific place, companies not only explicitly encourage relationship-building meetings but make them the norm."

If companies can do their part, it's also important for employees to get involved. For male leaders, that means making a particular effort to provide mentorship and sponsorship to junior female staff, even if that doesn't come naturally to them. "We tend to be drawn to people who are like ourselves and we're more comfortable socially interacting with similar others," Ragins says. "Although this may be a natural tendency, we need to recognize when it happens in ourselves and others, so that we can confront and change the behaviours."

For employees lower down the leadership food chain, they need to get comfortable with (diplomatically) calling out those male superiors who tend to provide mentorship only to other men. "They may not recognize when they're excluding women or they may be in deep denial," Ragins says.

And if that doesn't work? It's a radical step that might not be available to all women, but if they can, Ragins suggests looking for mentors elsewhere. "Polish off your résumé and find a place that values you."

> "*Fortune 500 companies with the highest proportion of women on their boards have shown to have significantly better performance than firms with the lowest proportion, and companies with higher gender diversity are more likely to have higher financial returns above their respective medians.*"

# The Glass Ceiling Limits Women in Business

*Tojan Rahhal*

*In the following viewpoint Tojan Rahhal discusses the so-called "glass ceiling" that limits women from advancing to the top tiers in organizations. She believes that this effect is very much in place even though we may not always see its sometimes-subtle effects. There are implicit biases in society that are often ingrained in the minds of male executives, such as the notion that women will not want to go on travel assignments. Rahhal believes that specific, necessary steps, such as supporting other women, can be taken to help women achieve more in the workplace. Tojan Rahhal is owner of Alliance Professional Development, where she conducts customized workshops on leadership development, cultural awareness, and professional skills.*

"Does the Glass Ceiling Exist? (Hint: Yes, It Does.)," by Tojan Rahhal, Columbia Business Times, May 4, 2017. Reprinted by permission.

As you read, consider the following questions:

1. Why is there ongoing debate about the existence of the glass ceiling?
2. How does mentoring factor into improved business situations for women?
3. Why is Rahhal optimistic about breaking the glass ceiling?

The term "glass ceiling" was coined in the early 1980s to describe the subtle—but very real—barriers that women and minorities in the workforce dealt with despite their qualifications. It's a sense that women or minorities, no matter how accomplished or capable, cannot reach the top-level jobs they might want.

There has been an ongoing debate on the existence of the glass ceiling. Some declare it doesn't exist because there are "women in power" and women have equal rights—therefore, any limits to their success must be self-created or self-perceived. But this argument doesn't account for the way society works for the Caucasian male: the way our implicit, natural biases associate CEO, millionaire, inventor, president, etc. with these men. We've been primed to limit a woman's reach and ability to climb the ladder in typically male-dominated fields.

As Jennifer Schenck, co-owner of the Connection Exchange, a local networking firm, says, the glass ceiling may not be as prevalent in "female-dominated career paths," but that doesn't mean that it's a negligible issue. There are nuances to limits women face as they advance in their careers, some of which aren't as visible, or aren't even intentional—they're a part of the natural biases that have built up in everyone, in part due to cultural and societal expectations of women.

Alyssa Liles-Amponsah, visual artist and associate director of K–12 programming in the Division of Inclusion, Diversity and Equity at MU, explains, "Just because the practice of marginalization is not always visible does not mean there aren't systemic obstacles

## RURAL WOMEN STRUGGLE WITH SEXUAL HARRASSMENT

A culture of male dominance in rural Australian workplaces is a key explainer for the high rate of sexual harassment.

Women in rural Australia experience workplace sexual harassment at alarming rates. Researchers Skype Saunders and Patricia Easteal interviewed 84 female employees from regional and remote areas of Western Australia, the Northern Territory, South Australia and New South Wales. They found that 73% of rural women had experienced sexual harassment at work. This is compared to 25% of women Australia-wide.

Only 35.7% of those surveyed said they would disclose incidents of sexual harassment. A culture of self-reliance, the effects of small town gossip, fewer employment opportunities, a workplace culture of victim blaming and geographic isolation from services (such as police and medical care) prohibited the reporting of sexual harassment.

Gender roles in rural Australia follow traditional patterns and this culture sets rural women as outsiders in the workplace.

Research argues that women in regional workplaces, traditionally dominated by men, face a range of behaviours that signal to them they do not belong and are intruding on male spaces. Sexual harassment is the most powerful of these.

41% of the agricultural workforce are female but in mining, only 16% of mining employees are women.

that are insidiously hidden that keep particular groups, like women, from advancing."

## Backing from Data

A study from Pay Scale found that women make 76 cents to the dollar a man earns, but that's just one manifestation of that systemic treatment that doesn't equate a woman's job with that of a man. There are far fewer women in the upper ranks of business, and a 2016 "Women in the Workplace" report from McKinsey & Company and Lean In showed that women deal with a slower

In workplaces where there are few women, women are more visible and they are more likely to experience hostility. Sexual harassment against women is more prevalent in male-dominated sectors such as mining and agriculture.

In rural towns where the line between private and public spheres is blurred, women's reporting of sexual harassment and discrimination can endanger their position in the social fabric of their communities.

For women seeking career progression in male-dominated sectors of rural Australia infiltrating the network of the "boys club" is seen as important. For example, one participant in a 2016 study stated that her career success depended on "drinking with the boys" at rural functions. She believed that opting out of events such as these would inhibit her career advancement.

Studies by Barbara Pini and Beatrice Dunfield found that women's access to leadership positions in agribusiness and agriculture was stifled by lower self-esteem due to systemic gender discrimination. In addition to sexual harassment Pini argued that workplaces did not support the balancing of work and family. She found leaders did not perceive female employees to have adequate skills and abilities and where there was culture of bullying, it inhibited women's access to leadership positions.

**"Women in Rural Workplaces Struggle Against the 'Boys Club' That Leads to Harassment," by Lucie Newsome, The Conversation, 02/28/2018. https://theconversation.com/women-in-rural-workplaces-struggle-against-the-boys-club-that-leads-to-harassment-92507. Licensed under CC BY-ND 4.0 International.**

rate of progress in their careers; as of 2016, only 19 percent of C-suite members were women. The Women in the Workplace study found that women entering the workforce "face more barriers to advancement than men at every level," and once in the company, they face "a steeper path to senior leadership.

Schenck recalls working for a large corporation in the '90s, where she was "called 'honey,' expected to make the coffee, and buy the daily paper for the boss while my male counterparts were out making sales calls," she says. Women routinely face these struggles in the workforce—they're given roles based on assumptions made by bosses who unknowingly make judgements against what a woman can or cannot do. A boss may assume that a female employee wouldn't be interested in projects involving travel, for example, depriving that woman of the opportunity at all.

Schenck says she had to prove herself until she was taken under the wings of male mentors, but she still noticed "more established female coworkers struggle to get the promotions," ultimately leaving for more diverse workplaces. Mentorship by company leaders, male or female, is one way to establish a supportive work environment that can lead to higher employee engagement and confidence in equal opportunities, which evidence suggests is better for the bottom line. Fortune 500 companies with the highest proportion of women on their boards have shown to have significantly better performance than firms with the lowest proportion, and companies with higher gender diversity are more likely to have higher financial returns above their respective medians. The culture of gender equality and inclusivity must be set at the top of the company to have a positive impact.

Schenck also points out that success means different things to different people—for men and for women, that may or may not include climbing the ladder. Nevertheless, it's important for companies to have a path to leadership with no gender bias. These biases are typically unconscious associations or cognitive shortcuts that have formed based on our exposure to images, media, and our environment—but they're malleable if one identifies and controls them.

## Inclusive Progress

When we talk about the glass ceiling, we must also account for the different vantage points. It's hard to reach the ceiling when you have no view of the top: you're stuck in the bottom of the pyramid, and that's the only example you've seen from people like you in the workplace. As Liles-Amponsah says, representation and role models are important to shaping the worldviews of young women. Therefore, being able to see yourself in a future "top of the pyramid" role can help erase the idea of a ceiling at all in a young woman's career pursuit.

Just as important is having men work on their natural biases—make decisions based on facts and performance and support an equitable workplace environment for all. For those at the top of the ladder, it's necessary to lead alongside others, helping bring them up along the way.

For those of us facing the glass ceiling, or aspiring to break it, we must avoid pessimism. Shape the policies and reach for our goals, no matter what they are. By supporting each other and being role models, we can eliminate any foreseen barriers. It won't be easy, but it is possible.

> "All I am trying to get across to these young women is that this so-called glass ceiling is imaginary, if only we women single-mindedly concentrate on achieving our vision and mission and work very hard to achieve the end goal."

# There Is No Such Thing as a Glass Ceiling

*Sumi Moonesinghe*

*In the following viewpoint Sumi Moonesinghe recounts her experience as an outlier in a man's world of science, technology, and business. She asserts that she never experienced harassment or prejudice due to her sex. Instead, male mentors, including her own husband, guided her career and her beliefs. She was allowed to work from home when necessary and obtained help where necessary. As a result, her company thrived. Moonesinghe believes all women can make the same luck for themselves in the business world if they keep working diligently. Sumi Moonesinghe is a prominent business leader in Sri Lanka.*

"There Is No Glass Ceiling as Such," by Sumi Moonesinghe, Daily FT (www.ft.lk), Wijeya Newspapers, March 9, 2018. Reprinted by permission.

As you read, consider the following questions:

1. How might Moonesinghe's experience be seen as merely anecdotal and not a reflection of what many women experience in the business world?
2. What "lucky" elements allowed Moonesinghe to thrive in the business world?
3. What suggestions does Moonesinghe have for helping other women succeed?

A t the age of 17 I decided to enter what was hitherto a man's world, by entering the Faculty of Engineering, University of Colombo, at the behest of my math and physics teacher—Mignon Lokubalasooriya, at Devi Balika Vidyalaya, Colombo 8.

I was the only girl in a batch of 104, and obtained a Bachelor's Degree in Electrical Engineering. There were 500 boys in the whole faculty! I am eternally indebted to my teacher for guiding my destiny.

I then proceeded to the Faculty of Electronics, University of Southampton in the UK and obtained a Master's Degree in Electronics. And once again I was the only woman, in all the faculties of engineering such as aeronautical, chemical, petroleum, civil mechanical and electrical, etc.

I then proceeded to Singapore as an expatriate lecturer in the Singapore Polytechnic to teach Colour television. Once again the only woman lecturer in the entire Faculty of Engineering.

During this entire period of 12 years I never encountered any glass ceilings or sexual harassment, nor did I ever ask for any concessions as a woman.

I was very confident, and learnt to handle sticky situations tactically. Everyone considered me as one of them and took care of me when the necessity arose.

I remember very vividly, once when I was on the main Peradeniya Gampola road doing surveying practicals in the hot sun, not even wearing a hat, when late Prof. E.O.E. Perera the then Dean of the Faculty of Engineering passing by, stopped the car to find out how I was doing. I never felt I should ask for any concessions from him as a woman.

I returned to Sri Lanka in 1974, and joined the Maharaja organisation as a director of a subsidiary company. I had no idea about business I was only a professional engineer. It was my late husband who taught me business, and shared my responsibilities at home, to become a very successful businesswoman.

My two bosses Ms. Maharaja and Raja Mahendran gave me all the encouragement and support and gave me a free hand to run the company.

I was the Founder/Managing Director of New Zealand Milk Products (now Fonterra Brands), selling Anchor milk powder/butter, etc. imported from New Zealand.

When I was expecting my second daughter, my gynaecologist, famous Dr. Henry Nanayakkara, very bluntly told me, "If you want this child, you have to stay in bed lying down, not even sitting down, for nine months!" I then decided, I am not ill, so I can manage this company from my bed at home. A very bold decision as there were no laptops, android phones but only telex and fax machines.

My two bosses were so kind they allowed me this enormous concession. And the company performed extremely well. None of my stakeholders in the business knew I was operating from my bed at home, thanks to my extremely efficient secretary June Jayakody.

In view of this performance they allowed me to work half a day, allowing me to be with my two daughters when they returned from school to help them with their studies. Both girls have excelled in their studies, not affected by a busy working mother!

Finally the company reached its pinnacle recording 70% market share, for Anchor and Ratthi milk powder brands, when it was sold to the New Zealand Dairy Board and I retired at the age of 51.

All I am trying to get across to these young women is that this so-called glass ceiling is imaginary, if only we women single-mindedly concentrate on achieving our vision and mission and work very hard to achieve the end goal.

Of course I was very lucky to have had a very caring husband (Susil Moonesinghe) and a younger sister who helped me to juggle between running a very large business, managing my home, attending to my two daughters' studies, and supporting my husband in his political journey as well.

I learnt to do five things at the same time and earned a reputation as a poor listener with a very short span of concentration! And a tough woman! I was gifted with this ability to be able to handle many things simultaneously.

So I call upon all heads of corporates to please understand the juggling women are expected to do, and allow them flexi hours, give them a laptop and android phone, and extended maternity leave and to work from home.

Today with advanced technology, you can conduct your business from anywhere, you only need a lap top and an android phone.

I call upon all women to be bold, confident and learn to juggle, and make your bosses feel comfortable that you will achieve the objectives laid down by them, from home, and single-mindedly concentrate on achieving! Then you will never encounter a glass ceiling.

Good luck! Every day is an International Women's Day!

> *"As I was working on this Keynote, it slowly dawned on me that I was being asked to present on empowering the vulnerable and promoting the identity of the oppressed as a ... White guy."*

# Men Must Confront Their Own White Male Privilege

David Gussak

*In the following viewpoint, David E. Gussak discusses his awakening to the knowledge that as a white man in a predominantly female field, art therapy, he has always had certain advantages. He admits that while he has knowledge in his field, he does not share the experiences of those he works with. Gussak vows to be more sensitive to his status as a privileged individual in society. He understands that by listening more to the concerns of others, particularly to those who do not share his privileged status, he can be more effective in his field and a better ally for the less privileged. David E. Gussak is chairperson of Florida State University's Department of Art Education and professor in its art therapy program.*

"Fighting My White Male Privilege—A Confession," by David Gussak, Sussex Publishers, November 1, 2016. Reprinted by permission.

As you read, consider the following questions:

1. Why does the author decide to rewrite his keynote speech?
2. How did the presidential debate between Clinton and Trump affect his thinking?
3. Why does the author admit that some people would not be happy with what he has written here?

I was preparing the Keynote address I would be delivering for the Canadian Art Therapy Association/Ontario Art Therapy Association Joint Conference on October 14th. The conference theme was Art Therapy and Anti-Oppressive Practice; my presentation "Drawing Out the Oppressed: Promoting Identity and Empowering the Vulnerable through Art Therapy" drew from my own work in one of the most oppressive environments—prison.

However, while I had spent months putting this together, I felt vaguely uneasy. And then, the Sunday before I was to deliver the Keynote, it occurred to me what was missing.

I was reviewing my PowerPoint while watching the second presidential debate. After the debate I became frustrated, embarrassed, self-conscious. I spent 90 minutes watching a self-described alpha male justifying his nasty statements about women as locker room talk, watched him lurk closely behind her in what I perceived as a threatening and domineering manner. And, many people excused it simply because he was a strong white man.

As a white man, I felt part of the system that allowed this to happen. I looked down at my notes. I realized what seemed off; speaking about anti-oppressive practice without addressing my own identity felt disingenuous. So I re-wrote my introduction.

The conference audience held hundreds of people, the majority of which were women. This is common in our field; the latest numbers recognize that well over 90 percent of art therapists are women.

I began the presentation with a slide on the screen of a large elephant:

"My presentation is called Drawing out the Oppressed: Promoting Identity and Empowering the Vulnerable." And yet, as I look around this room and consider our field at large, I need to call attention to what I perceive as a fairly large elephant in the room.

You see, I recognize that those who oppress are usually self-perceived as part of the dominant culture, the top of an apparent hierarchy established by the society to which we belong.

Now, this brings me to [this] elephant ...

I don't know if you know this or not, but I am going to tell you something very personal about myself ... something many people may not know ...

Here it is.

[I whispered] I'm a white guy

As I was working on this Keynote, it slowly dawned on me that I was being asked to present on empowering the vulnerable and promoting the identity of the oppressed as a...

... White guy

And even more so, a white guy from the United States

I am being asked to focus on a topic that many recognize—in my opinion correctly—that those who share my identity actually contribute to the disparities and disproportions common in our society.

While I haven't always recognized this, I have come to see it recently, particularly over the last few years, and dare I say it—clearly during this latest election occurring just south of all of you...[oh, and by the way, given the comments made by one of the presidential candidates about Canada—I'm sorry; we don't all feel like that]

I do indeed recognize the hypocrisy.

And, I also confess, while my awareness of white male privilege has emerged slowly over the years, there has risen my own recognition that I—and my ilk—represent and promote the power imbalance inherent in many of our countries and cultures.

Granted, you do have Trudeau [prime minister of Canada], and might I add, how very jealous I am …

Please bear with me; I feel I need to say this before I begin the actual topic at hand—I felt I couldn't be honest unless I recognize the position of power from which I work.

I bring this up to neither apologize nor brag—while being a white man doesn't provide me any greater insight it doesn't conversely negate my position …

I point all this out so that we can work through this conspicuous and inconvenient truth and segue into relating the difficult and challenging work that we—or I—experience as an art therapist providing services for those who are oppressed, either by dominant cultures or by dominant justice systems.

I have had to keep all this in my mind that despite my attempt to overcome the disparities, to acknowledge and recognize the oppression within our given cultures, I am speaking from observation and very little from direct experience.

But I have seen it and I acknowledge it.

So, let me begin …"

By learning there are multiple perspectives, not just one put forth by the dominant paradigm, I am more likely to recognize that I don't know what the other person is experiencing, and therefore can indeed be more effective—as a therapist, teacher, professional.

Don't get me wrong. My own sense of superiority developed through my position of privilege continues to raise its ugly head at the most inopportune times—but I am getting better at recognizing it. It is a continuous effort.

At first, when people would tell me, "you cannot possibly understand where we are coming from as you are perceiving this from a position of privilege" I would get my hackles up; they don't know me—I had no privileges growing up.

I had struggles; I had challenges. I didn't always have money. I had difficulty in school; I worried about work. As a Jewish man, I have encountered forms of anti-Semitism and racist bigotry. But, years ago, a colleague once described me as a member of "an invisible minority." While I took affront to that then, I seem to now understand what he meant.

I carried the most obvious and visible of privileges.

Yes, some perceive that as a "male art therapist" I must know what it feels like to be part of a minority.

However, while I am a white man in what Gladys Agell (Fago, 1989) described as a women's field, I am part of a women's field in what is societally still perceived as a man's world.

Yes, I have had to overcome some things to get where I am. Yet, a person of color, a woman, beginning with the same limitations would have so much more to overcome, would require a great deal more energy, time, luck, before arriving at a similar place. For some, it may even take generations. Even when "arriving", their positions might still be suspect, that they succeeded because of who they knew, legislation that "favored" them, reluctant opportunities provided out of guilt and obligation.

Yet, no one would suspect me.

Let's be honest. I don't have to be afraid walking home alone at night. I don't have to worry about what may occur when I get pulled over. My salary is based on my merit and worth, not limited because of my gender or identity.

Previous posts have examined the question of identity—my own as an art therapist, and those with whom I serve. In order to provide the work that I do, in prison, I recognize that there is a hierarchical imbalance, and that part of my job is to help those inside create new identities and labels, to once again take back power, and rise above the identity of that of "inmate".

Yet, I left out this most important piece. I was reluctant to do so. Even now, I must confess, writing this blog has been daunting.

I read a recent article in The New Yorker in which author George Packer examined some of the tasks Hillary Clinton has had—and will have—in bridging the ever widening gaps between white America, and…well… everyone else.

Packer acknowledged that many people—particularly some who are more left-leaning—feel their white identity precluded them from discussing race and identity. On some level they felt they had no right to bring up that which they helped create.

"If racial injustice is considered to be monolithic and unchanging—omitting the context of individual actions, white and black—the political response tends to be equally rigid—genuflection or rejection. Clinton's constituency surely includes many voters who would welcome a nuanced discussion on race… But identity politics breaks down the distinction between an idea and the person articulating it, so that before speaking up one has to ask: Does my identity give me the right to say this? This atmosphere makes honest conversation very hard, and gives a demagogue like Trump the aura of truth-teller … when people of good will are afraid to air legitimate arguments the illegitimate kind gains power" (2016, pg. 56)

While Packer focused on the color of one's skin, the argument extends to sex, gender identity and religion as well. We are reluctant to admit this out loud because we are afraid of how we may sound. Or, let me own this—I am reluctant to admit this …

Packer, in a few paragraphs later, seems to let us off the hook. Restating what social scientist Glenn Lowry of Brown University said, "the new racial politics actually asks little of sympathetic whites: a confession, a reading assignment" (2016, p.56).

Perhaps this is my first step in contributing to the discussion of racial politics—my own written assignment.

Certainly, some may find this post disingenuous, written from a position of superiority, and people on both sides of the issue may take umbrage to my statements.

Some could argue—and perhaps rightly so—why is it that a white man can get away with making these statements but if a woman or a person of color does so, he or she is complaining, is rocking the boat, is picking a fight?

I don't know really know why, but I suspect it is likely because of what Clinton referred to as implicit bias.

To that, I ask that you accept the message and don't condemn the messenger.

As an art therapist in prison, I have primarily worked with inmates of different color and background.

As a professor of art therapy, I have taught classes made up mostly of women.

As a chair of a department in a large state university I represent and answer to many people of diverse and varied backgrounds and experiences.

As a professional art therapist, lecturing, holding office, running committees, I represent a field of which I am only one of a handful of men.

For years, I have taught theories derived mostly from Western Eurocentric perspectives, not recognizing that when Jung refers to "primitive cultures" this is derogatory to certain cultures and identities. The white male dominant perspective influenced even the women who have founded and shaped our field. This needs to change.

I have learned to be aware of my identity, and from whence and to whom I speak. I have also come to accept, albeit slowly at times, that I do not always come from a position of understanding.

Like I indicated in the Keynote's introduction, I speak from observation but very little from experience.

However, in order to be an ally, it is important to listen to people who have experience with racism and structural oppression. I am not always good at this, but I am learning to listen and to accept I don't have all the answers.

But I have seen the disparities, and I acknowledge it.

> *"I refused to say #MeToo, not because I've never dealt with abuses of power, but because I have and wouldn't voluntarily grant anyone the opportunity to contemplate my humiliation or dismiss me as a mere victim."*

# Privileged Males Have Fought Back Against #MeToo

*Ephrat Livni*

*In the following viewpoint, Ephrat Livni writes of the backlash against the #MeToo movement, and how men, ever the dominant cultural force, have stolen victimhood away from the very women who have been victimized. After a year of male silence following the Harvey Weinstein revelations, men have fought back with a vengeance. Livni cites the cases of Supreme Court Justice Brett Kavanaugh and writer Stephen Elliot, both of whom have claimed to be the victims in their stories. Livni believes that women must fight back, work their way into positions of power, and flip the script. Ephrat Livni is a writer and lawyer. She has written for the Jerusalem Report, ABC News, and FindLaw, served in the Peace Corps in Senegal, taught English in Japan, was a public defender in Palm Beach County, and worked as an attorney at Google in Silicon Valley.*

"There's a Problem at the Heart of #MeToo—Here's How to Solve It," by Ephrat Livni, Republished with permission of Quartz Media LLC, October 14, 2018. Permission conveyed through Copyright Clearance Center, Inc..

As you read, consider the following questions:

1. What does the author believe is the problem with the #MeToo movement as it has played out over the past few years?
2. How have Brett Kavanaugh and Stephen Elliot fought back against their accusers, according to the viewpoint?
3. What other evidence does the author offer that men have refused to acknowledge their wrongs and have fought back against female empowerment?

One year ago, people got woke—or so the story goes. After the *New York Times* and the *New Yorker* revealed a slew of sexual assault and sexual misconduct allegations against Hollywood producer Harvey Weinstein, countless women were moved to share their personal experiences of harassment and abuse on social media under the hashtag #MeToo. A movement was born.

#MeToo made me nervous. While it's imperative to eradicate abuse, it seemed to me then that women were falling into a dangerous trap, sharing tales of our subjugation and humiliation for the titillation of a culture ultimately indifferent to women's dignity or safety.

I refused to say #MeToo, not because I've never dealt with abuses of power, but because I have and wouldn't voluntarily grant anyone the opportunity to contemplate my humiliation or dismiss me as a mere victim. And I worried that as #MeToo unfolded, it was playing into an ancient narrative written by men, for men. In this story, if women are to be heard at all, it's only when we talk about men and sex.

If the hashtag had been less polite—a rebel yell like #F***You—I might have found it more inspiring. Still, after a while, I got used to the idea that sharing our horror stories might somehow lead to recognition of our inherent equality. Women seemed galvanized and unified by the hashtag activism. I wondered if I'd been impatient, wanting to skip steps and get to the part where we're all humans instead of acknowledging the need for course correction.

Maybe, I thought, #MeToo was provoking change after all. Not only had mighty men fallen from lofty positions when their wrongs were exposed, but the idea that power abuses are a common problem seemed ensconced in the cultural conversation.

Now, in the wake of Brett Kavanaugh's confirmation to the US Supreme Court and other recent events, once again, I'm not so sure. It seems that the story of #MeToo has turned into yet another opportunity for men to talk about themselves—how they've suffered as a result of accusations, or redeemed themselves and deserve our attention again, or how the world's gone mad and lost its standards, or how they are allies and not bad guys. Whatever the response, men retain cultural dominance, so much so that a man like Kavanaugh, accused of attempted rape, can trigger fears that boys won't get to be boys anymore if women keep telling their stories.

## Change We Can Believe In?

Change happens—unevenly. In 1991, Clarence Thomas was confirmed to the Supreme Court despite testimony from lawyer Anita Hill, who accused Thomas of sexual harassment before an an all-male Senate Judiciary Committee. The next year, in 1992, more women ran for political office and were elected to the Senate than ever before. It was dubbed The Year of the Woman.

Now history seems to be repeating itself. This year, Kavanaugh was confirmed to the high court despite testimony from Christine Blasey Ford, who alleged that Kavanaugh had tried to rape her in high school. Kavanaugh appeared both outraged and entitled in his own Senate testimony—an emotional response that perfectly encapsulated the backlash to #MeToo. Indeed, Jia Tolentino at *The New Yorker* argues that Kavanaugh was confirmed because of #MeToo: "Men are borrowing the rhetoric of the structurally oppressed," she writes, "and delivering it with a rage that is denied to all but the most powerful."

In other words, powerful men are coopting the unassailable position of victim and advancing it with the brutality of oppressors. When women accuse men of sexual misconduct, the accused and their allies rewrite the narrative. They create a scenario in which they have been wronged by a hysterical culture, and in which their accusers are either malicious or hopelessly befuddled. (Kavanaugh supporters, including the judge himself, were typically reluctant to say that Ford was lying about being assaulted, preferring instead to suggest that she had somehow confused her assailant with someone else.)

Kavanaugh was the perfect avatar for all the privileged men who are sick and tired of #MeToo. For a whole year, they've been told to tread with caution and wrestle with self-doubt. They're not going to take it anymore, and they're telling us a different story.

## Woe Is Men

Another aggrieved man is the writer Stephen Elliot, whose name appeared on last year's S***ty Media Men List—a spreadsheet meant to warn women in the industry away from men accused of sexual harassment, abuse, and other forms of boundary-crossing. On Oct. 10, Elliot filed a defamation lawsuit, claiming that Moira Donegan and other anonymous women had knowingly destroyed his reputation with anonymous false rape accusations. Elliot's defense, presented in the legal filing and in an essay in Quillete describing his experiences since the list was made public, is that he couldn't possibly rape or harass women because he doesn't even like sex.

Elliot points to his own nonfiction writing about being a submissive in erotic practices known as Bondage Dominance Sadism Masochism (BDSM). He writes in Quillette:

> My entire sexuality is wrapped up in BDSM. Cross-dressing, bondage, masochism. I'm always the bottom. I've been in long romantic relationships with women without ever seeing them naked. Almost every time I've had intercourse during the past 10 years, it has been in the context of dominance/submission,

often without my consent, and usually while I'm tied up or in a straitjacket and hood.

In his essay, he attempts to transform himself from alleged predator to unwary prey, targeted by vicious women who "weaponized" their baseless hate. He accuses the women behind the Media List of intellectual dishonesty as he disingenuously conflates the involuntary non-consensual sex alleged against him—the crime of rape noted on the spreadsheet—with his own voluntary erotic activities, which, frankly, in no way reassures me Elliot's not a creep. The "non-consensual sex" Elliot has in the context of BDSM is actually consensual, as he's apparently agreed to be tied up and placed in a straitjacket or hood as he submits to domination. That's hardly the same thing as sex without consent. His use of the term, his mere mention of this to elicit some kind of image of himself as a victim, is ridiculous.

Elliot's essay is focused on his suffering. He applies legal concepts, like the notion of being innocent until proven guilty, to discuss his loss of cultural status, calling the scenario created by the list "Kafkaesque." Proof of this is that his latest book wasn't widely reviewed. His writing was rejected by major publications. He took drugs, became depressed, spent his savings, lost allies, was forced to reconsider his purpose, to move from expensive LA to affordable Louisiana, to return to writing for its own sake rather than for glory and lucre.

It's true that the list was problematic because, while it was created as a secret document, it quickly became public. Donnegan, its creator, herself admitted that it took on a life of its own which she never intended.

What Elliot fails to realize, however, is that he was never entitled to publication, book reviews, success, wealth, or friendship—either before or after the list. He was briefly blessed and then quickly dismissed. It's not nice for him, but it's hardly a shocking or unique experience, nor is it a sign of a society gone terribly awry.

# Welcome to the World

Elliot's shock at the experience of falling out of cultural favor is just a sign of the privilege he's enjoyed until now. For the many intelligent and talented women whose dreams of greatness and recognition have been hampered by an accident of birth, working in a world unwilling to fully recognize their potential—not to mention unfairness, doubt, rejection, double standards, lower pay, and insufficient respect—is just the way things go.

Elliot's lawsuit may not succeed. But the timing of his filing, on the heels of Kavanaugh's confirmation, is one more sign of how the tides have turned against #MeToo. As senator Lindsey Graham said in defense of the patriarchy after Kavanaugh's testimony earlier in the month, "I'm a single white male from South Carolina, and I'm told that I should just shut up, but I will not shut up."

# Year of the Man

Evidence of this refusal to shut up abounds. As if on cue, just ahead of the one-year mark of the #MeToo movement, a slew of accused men reentered the cultural conversation. Louis CK, who admitted to masturbating in front of women comics, began making impromptu appearances at the Comedy Cellar. Aziz Ansari, accused more of being a creep than a criminal, popped up again with a comedy routine that decries the excesses of wokeness. Jian Ghomeshi, a Canadian radio personality accused of multiple abuses, wrote a self-pitying essay for the New York Review of Books, defended by then-editor Ian Buruma, who felt the time had come to test the boundaries of #MeToo. Disgraced radio host John Hockenberry also wrote an essay in Harper's mourning the end of romance and calling himself an "exile." The list goes on.

While there's still a lot of rhetoric about supporting women being bandied about, there's an equal and opposite reaction to #MeToo happening now. The culture may believe that women like Ford can be victims, but people still feel deeply for men in power. And men still dominate industries, institutions, and cultural production, which means the most they're willing to offer women is lip service. As Lindsay Zoladz writes in The Ringer, discussing male artists' recent penchant for making "oddly soulless" songs in tribute to strong women, "In so many aspects of our culture, 2018 has been the year of women's rage. On the radio and on the charts, though, 2018 has been the year of the benevolent-yet-patronizing women's empowerment anthem, as imagined by men."

The powerful do not cede space willingly, and certainly not to victims. And so, although I hope that 2019 will be the Year of the Woman, I fear that it will be, like every year preceding it and many that will follow, just another Year of the Man.

A culture reluctant to be disrupted will only transform when women say #MeToo not about abuse but our right to rule, and say #F***You to anyone who refuses us opportunities. We have to work our way into the powerful positions where the dominant narrative is written, and create a new kind of script.

> *"Writing in the Globe and Mail,*
> *Atwood said the #MeToo movement,*
> *which emerged in the wake of sexual*
> *assault allegations against Hollywood*
> *producer Harvey Weinstein, was the*
> *symptom of a broken legal system*
> *and had been seen as a massive wake*
> *up call."*

# There Are Flaws in #MeToo

*Ashifa Kassam*

*In the following viewpoint Ashifa Kassam writes of the controversy surrounding Canadian novelist and feminist Margaret Atwood (The Handmaid's Tale), who defended a male professor friend accused of sexual impropriety. Her call for due process for the professor was met with resistance by those in the #MeToo movement. Atwood counters that "innocent until proven guilty" is a hallmark of our civilized society and that vigilante justice is the sign of a broken system. For Atwood, defending basic civil rights was not equivalent to warring against women, but many feminists were not convinced. Ashifa Kassam is the Canada correspondent for* Guardian US.

"Margaret Atwood Faces Feminist Backlash on Social Media over #MeToo," by Ashifa Kassam, Guardian News and Media Limited, January 15, 2018. Reprinted by permission.

As you read, consider the following questions:

1. What are Margaret Atwood's concerns with the #MeToo movement?
2. In what ways have women reacted to her defense of the professor accused of sexual misconduct?
3. What alternatives does Atwood list as to how society might move forward in the age of #MeToo?

Canadian author Margaret Atwood is facing a social media backlash after voicing concerns about the #MeToo movement and calling for due process in the case of a former university professor accused of sexual misconduct.

Writing in the Globe and Mail, Atwood said the #MeToo movement, which emerged in the wake of sexual assault allegations against Hollywood producer Harvey Weinstein, was the symptom of a broken legal system and had been "seen as a massive wake up call".

However, she wondered where North American society would go from here. "If the legal system is bypassed because it is seen as ineffectual, what will take its place? Who will be the new power brokers?" Atwood asked.

She raised the possibility that the answer could leave women divided. "In times of extremes, extremists win. Their ideology becomes a religion, anyone who doesn't puppet their views is seen as an apostate, a heretic or a traitor, and moderates in the middle are annihilated."

The 78-year-old author of *The Handmaid's Tale* drew a parallel between these concerns and those who accused her of being a "bad feminist" after she signed an open letter last year calling for due process for a University of British Columbia professor facing allegations of sexual misconduct.

The university's administration released few details on the case against Steven Galloway, the former chair of the creative writing program, saying only that he was facing "serious allegations". After a months-long investigation he was fired, but the official findings were never released. The faculty association said in a statement that all but one of the allegations, including the most serious allegation, were not substantiated.

In her piece, Atwood pointed to the university's lack of transparency around the allegations and noted that Galloway had been asked to sign a confidentiality agreement.

"The public—including me—was left with the impression that this man was a violent serial rapist, and everyone was free to attack him publicly, since under the agreement he had signed, he couldn't say anything to defend himself," she wrote. "A fair-minded person would now withhold judgment as to guilt until the report and the evidence are available for us to see."

She likened the affair to the Salem witch trials, in that guilt was assumed of those who were accused. This idea of guilt by accusation had at times been used to usher in a better world or justify new forms of oppression, she wrote. "But understandable and temporary vigilante justice can morph into a culturally solidified lynch-mob habit, in which the available mode of justice is thrown out the window, and extralegal power structures are put into place and maintained."

Many online took issue with her view. "If @MargaretAtwood would like to stop warring amongst women, she should stop declaring war against younger, less powerful women and start listening," wrote one person on Twitter. "In today's dystopian news: One of the most important feminist voices of our time shits on less powerful women to uphold the power of her powerful male friend," wrote another.

Some accused Atwood of using her position of power to silence those who had come forward with allegations against Galloway. "'Unsubstantiated' does not mean innocent. It means there was not enough evidence to convict," read one tweet.

Others defended Atwood. "Genuinely upsetting to see Margaret Atwood attacked for pointing out that 'innocent until proven guilty' is the key to a civilised society. That has to still be a thing, yes? How can that suddenly be a bad thing?"

In a statement to the Guardian, Atwood pointed to the Universal Declaration of Human Rights, echoing an earlier tweet in which she defended her view by noting that endorsing basic human rights for everyone was not equivalent to warring against women.

Her opinion piece, she said, was meant to highlight the choice we now face; fix the system, bypass it or "burn the system down and replace it with, presumably, another system".

> "The sisterhood is now global. And there's no doubt that the mood has changed. Assaults on women that were commonplace but not acknowledged are now put in the public domain and challenged. But we have to learn the right lessons from these moments."

# It Is Time for Women to Confront Male Privilege

*Harriet Harman*

*In the following viewpoint, Harriet Harman examines the fallout from the revelations that numerous high-powered men were using their status to act inappropriately with women. Harmon sets out a list of key takeaways, lessons that society must learn in the wake of such news. Harman relates the sexual imbalance to that of pay scales for men and women, observing that there is a substantial pay gap between what male and female employees of the BBC are paid for example. In both cases, Harman suggests that women must be dogged and determined in their pursuit of equal rights because male privilege is deeply entrenched in society. Harriet Harman is a British solicitor and Labour Party politician who has served as a member of Parliament since 1982.*

"Time for Women to Take on Male Privilege," by Harriet Harman, Guardian News and Media Limited, February 22, 2018. Reprinted by permission.

As you read, consider the following questions:

1. How has social media empowered women when it comes to standing up for themselves?
2. What lessons does Harman take away from recent events that have exposed male sexual impropriety?
3. How does Harman relate sexual impropriety to the pay gap for men and women?

We're having an extended series of "moments" about gender with Harvey Weinstein's outing as a serial sexual assaulter, outrage at United States President Donald Trump's celebration of groping women and the rise of #metoo and #timesup.

Social media allows women around the world to immediately see how their sisters are battling to make progress. The women's movement which, in decades gone by, flourished around kitchen tables and at school gates is now—courtesy the internet—international.

An affront to women in the US engenders support in the United Kingdom, the passionate misogyny speech of Julia Gillard, former prime minister of Australia, inspired solidarity and anger in the UK. The sisterhood is now global. And there's no doubt that the mood has changed. Assaults on women that were commonplace but not acknowledged are now put in the public domain and challenged. But we have to learn the rights lessons from these moments.

The first is that we've made progress. In years past, Weinstein would have been regarded as frisky, "a bit of a lad", the young women judged as "asking for it" or frigid. Now it is acknowledged as wrong and it is the men who have to account for their actions rather than the women they prey on.

Second, Weinstein is not "one bad apple". That sort of behaviour is prevalent in the film industry and indeed in all occupations with a male hierarchy and in which women want to advance. The vast majority of men would not dream of abusing their power to force themselves on young women. But some will and hitherto they've had impunity.

Third, the lesson is that there's safety in numbers. One woman on her own would just have been crushed by Weinstein's powerful legal and PR team and driven out of the industry. But no man can do that when there are a multitude of women's voices.

Fourth, we need to use the moment to challenge men acting in the same way. Women, and men, have been doing that in respect of other men in the film industry. In the UK, women stood up to challenge a cabinet minister, defence secretary Michael Fallon. Jayne Merrick, a young journalist, risked her reputation and her career to speak up about Fallon groping her. But others then came forward and he was sacked.

Fifth, we need to alter the complaints system so that a man who sexually assaults women is stopped after the first occasion not only after decades. That means the complainant must be able to report anonymously. No woman wants to be known only for the fact that she's complained against a famous man.

There must be independent adjudication of complaints. He can't be judged by people who know and work with him, but don't know her. And there must be protection from backlash and discrimination against the victim. The complainant is doing a public service by challenging criminality. She must be protected—not vilified. In the UK, parliament is changing its rules for complaints against MPs, as is the Labour Party.

Six, we need to ensure that male-dominated hierarchies are a thing of the past. Sexual assault and exploitation cannot thrive in the same way where there is a mixed team of men and women in authority.

In more rumbling in the gender jungle, there has been an explosion of anger and embarrassment in the UK about unequal pay triggered by the BBC. We all love "Auntie", as Britain's national broadcaster is known, but it is not at all lovable that the BBC pays its on-screen men massively more than its women.

Carrie Gracie, the brilliant Mandarin-speaking BBC Chinese editor, discovered that she was paid 50 per cent less than the BBC's US editor. (And he doesn't have to speak Mandarin or risk arrest to do his job). She protested and resigned and BBC women and the wider women's movement rallied to her support.

There is need for Britain's Equality and Human Rights Commission (EHRC) to collate and publish this information by sector and by region so all women, and men, can see how their organisation compares. And the EHRC will need to insist on tough action plans and strict targets. Unions will need to move pay equality up the bargaining agenda to do justice for their female members. We don't just want to see the gender pay gap, we want to change it.

Success in the battle to get a pay gap reporting into law was swiftly followed by heated argument about how it would be measured. I held out for average hourly pay for women compared to average hourly pay for men. That way, we'll be able to see the discrimination against the army of female part-time workers. Britain's National Office of Statistics has reported the pay gap as around 9 per cent—a figure which I've never believed.

Early reports from organisations publishing ahead of the April deadline show it around 30 per cent, which I think will be nearer the mark. We can celebrate that we've changed the mood. But we need to change the reality and that means change in policy and processes. Male privilege is deeply entrenched. These "gender moments" put that in the spotlight. But they mustn't be just movements. We must use them as the spur to change and that means relentless persistence and dogged determination. But with the support women can gain from each other around the world, we are up to the task.

# Periodical and Internet Sources Bibliography

*The following articles have been selected to supplement the diverse views presented in this chapter.*

Lindsay Border, "Women: Are We to Blame for the Glass Ceiling?" Oct. 16, 2013. https://www.entrepreneur.com/article/229389

Catherine Fox, "Getting men on board is part of the solution to female disadvantage at work." *Guardian.* June 14, 2014. https://www.theguardian.com/sustainable-business/2017/jun/15/getting-men-on-board-is-part-of-the-solution-to-female-disadvantage-at-work

Joel Hilleker, "Why White Male Privilege Helps Nobody." The Trumpet. March 20, 2019. https://www.thetrumpet.com/18798-why-white-male-privilege-helps-nobody

Ruchir Joshi, "A revolution against male privilege." Oct. 25, 2018. *Telegraph.* https://www.telegraphindia.com/opinion/a-revolution-against-male-privilege/cid/1672495

Audrey S. Lee, "How to break up the old boys' club in your office." Quartz. Apr. 8, 2014. https://qz.com/196273/how-to-break-up-the-old-boys-club-in-your-office/

Thomas Page McBee, "Kendrick Sampson on Masculinity, Race, and Why Men Should Be More Vulnerable." *Teen Vogue.* March 26, 2019. https://www.teenvogue.com/story/kendrick-sampson-masculinity-race-vulnerable

Robert Merry, "The War Over 'Toxic Masculinity.'" *American Conservative.* January 23, 2019. https://www.theamericanconservative.com/articles/the-war-over-toxic-masculinity/

Caren Scheepers and Shireen Chengadu, "There Is No Glass Ceiling." Acumen. Jan 3, 2018. https://www.acumenmagazine.co.za/articles/there-is-no-glass-ceiling-6885.html

Ben Shapiro, "The 'Toxic Masculinity' Smear." *National Review.* June 7, 2017. https://www.nationalreview.com/2017/06/masculinity-not-toxic-stop-blaming-men-everything/

"White Privilege Does Not Exist," Hotep Nation. April 27, 2019. https://www.hotepnation.com/white-privilege-not-exist/

Friska Wirya, "There is no glass ceiling, there is a sticky floor." 30 March, 2017. https://www.acumenmagazine.co.za/articles/there-is-no-glass-ceiling-6885.html

Natalie Wolfe, "Strategies used by men 'scared' of #MeToo movement could be negatively affecting women." News.com.au. Dec. 7, 2018. https://www.news.com.au/finance/work/at-work/strategies-used-by-men-scared-of-metoo-movement-could-be-negatively-affecting-women/news-story/42d945a126b5a3d2d4f97f41374732d4

OPPOSING
VIEWPOINTS®
SERIES

CHAPTER 4

# What Steps Can Be Taken to Even the Playing Field?

# Chapter Preface

In general, people don't like change, and people in power like it even less. Despite numerous calls to ensure more rights for those in marginalized groups, such as racial and ethnic minorities, women, LGBQ individuals, and others, most societies have resisted such efforts. It is difficult enough to get those in the power structure to recognize their privilege; getting them to give it up or at least bring others along with them is doubly hard.

Consider for example, the Equal Rights Amendment (ERA). According to a website supporting this legislation, "The Equal Rights Amendment is a proposed amendment to the United States Constitution designed to guarantee equal legal rights for all American citizens regardless of sex; it seeks to end the legal distinctions between men and women in terms of divorce, property, employment, and other matters."

One would think that such legislation would breeze through Congress. After all, the United States was founded on the concept that all men are created equal, endowed by their creator with certain unalienable rights, and that among these are life, liberty, and the pursuit of happiness.

Of course, a key point here is how one interprets the word "men." Is it "mankind," or just the male sex? In any event, the attempt to pass an Equal Rights Amendment has a long tortuous history. The first version of the amendment was introduced by women's rights leader Alice Paul in 1923. But legislation being itself a slow process, a reworked version of the original amendment didn't pass the House of Representatives and the Senate until 1972. As is true of all amendments, it was then sent to the states for ratification. Because the threshold for ratification is so high—three-fourths of the fifty states have to sign on—the ERA was not ratified in the seven year deadline that Congress had laid out for it. As of today, 36 of the needed 38 states have ratified the ERA, and so it remains in limbo, and women's constitutional rights are still not protected. The states that have obstructed the ERA's progress are Alabama, Arizona, Arkansas, Florida, Georgia, Illinois, Louisiana, Mississippi, Missouri, Nevada, North Carolina, Oklahoma, South Carolina, Utah, and Virginia.

The same lethargy and obstruction has hindered the fight for racial equality in the United States.

Take, for example, the history of affirmative action, policies which seek to level the playing field for those who have traditionally been discriminated against. Though affirmative action in hiring practices was signed into law in the United States by President John F. Kennedy in 1961, it has been the subject of numerous court challenges in the years afterward. These challenges have concerned the college admissions process, where affirmative action has enabled a larger number of minority candidates to gain acceptance at universities. For example, the University of Michigan was sued on several occasions by students who believed that the school's affirmative action policies had favored minority candidates over themselves. This led to the approval by voters of Proposal 2—also called the Michigan Civil Rights Initiative. Passed in 2006, this law banned public institutions from discriminating against or giving preferential treatment to groups or individuals based on their race, gender, color, ethnicity, or national origin. Minority enrollment at the University of Michigan dropped precipitously, and left administrators scrambling to find ways to admit minority candidates. But in 2016, an affirmative action system used by the University of Texas survived another such challenge, as the Supreme Court by a 4-3 majority allowed the school to continue considering race in admissions decisions.

The narrowness of that decision demonstrates just how tenuous policies to level the playing field are in today's contentious society.

Getting the powers-that-be to acknowledge privilege is one matter; getting them to do something is an entirely different challenge. As Jamie Utt observes, when those in the power structure acknowledge their privilege, they may feel that such an admission is enough, and not feel the need to help dismantle the system that created their privilege. "If acknowledging privilege at a surface level enables those with privilege to avoid the radical work of ceding power and working in solidarity, it gives us an out from actually doing justice work," she writes.

Those who work for social justice understand that real progress cannot be made until those in power get on board. In a country where over 40 percent of voters support the privilege-driven policies of a conservative administration, this progress may come more slowly than ever.

| "*I have come to believe that any time we ask people from marginalized groups to focus on self-responsibility at the very time when they are taking the enormous risk of speaking truthfully of their experience rather than hiding it, we are reinforcing the very power differences that they are inviting us to look at.*" |

# Privileged People Should Listen to Criticism Without Overreacting

*Miki Kashtan*

*In the following viewpoint, Miki Kashtan writes that we have the power to shape our own thoughts and control our life, even in extremely difficult circumstances. As a privileged member of society, she applies this knowledge to working with marginalized groups. Kashtan believes that with privilege comes responsibility. This includes the ability to listen to criticism from the less-privileged and not react emotionally to how the criticism is stated, even if it is stated bluntly or inappropriately. Hearing the message is more important and will lead to healthier relationships and a freer society. Miki Kashtan is a cofounder of Bay Area Nonviolent Communication and lead collaboration consultant at the Center for Efficient Collaboration. Her articles have appeared in the* New York Times, Tikkun, *and elsewhere.*

"Privilege, Responsibility, and Nonviolence," by Miki Kashtan, Sussex Publishers, July 15, 2017. Reprinted by permission.

As you read, consider the following questions:

1. What does the author mean in saying that the actions of another person are a stimulus and not a cause for one's feelings?
2. Why does the author include the passage about Etty Hillesum?
3. What dynamic does the author lay out that she sees repeatedly in interactions between privileged and marginalized people?

When I first heard Marshall Rosenberg, back in 1994, say that the actions of another person are a stimulus, and never a cause, for my feelings, I was shocked. Little did I know that this statement would become the nucleus of my growing understanding about what has come to be called self-responsibility in the community of practice that I belong to: those who have chosen to adopt Nonviolent Communication (NVC) as a core organizing principle of our lives and work. This is a spiritual practice that is surprisingly demanding in moments when it's so tempting to think that I am having the experience I am having, or that I am doing what I doing, because of what someone else is doing or some other force that is outside me. Locating the source of my inner experience and my choices within me has been the most difficult and most liberating aspect of my practice.

Equally liberating, and far less comfortable, has been the twin practice of taking responsibility for my actions and choices and their effects within an interdependent world. The juxtaposition of the two conjures up mystery: my actions, however harmful they may be, don't cause the feelings of another, nor are their feelings unrelated to my actions. The nature of the relationship is elusive and complex, as all interdependence is. When you add power differences to the mix, responsibility, all around, becomes an achievement few of us can step into fully, without blame of self or other. Teasing apart this complexity is one of the ways I aim to use whatever privilege I have in the world in service of transforming the structures and effects of privilege.

## Self-Responsibility in the Absence of Power

When Etty Hillesum left the transitional camp near Amsterdam and went, ahead of her "turn," to Auschwitz to die during World War II, she dropped a note from the train, the last piece of her writing we are aware of. What she wrote was: "We left the camp singing". The published parts of her diary, titled *An Interrupted Life,* describe a journey towards more and more self-responsibility of the kind I am talking about here in a world that was closing in on her, giving her fewer and fewer external options. Etty understood more and more pointedly that no one could take away from her the ultimate power we each have: the choice of what we tell ourselves about what is happening. She understood and was able to demonstrate in her writings that no event "makes" us feel this way or that way; that we are the creators of our inner experience through how we make meaning of what happens. She reached the point of knowing that she could choose how to act in the most extreme of circumstances, up against the most concentrated form of hatred known. In that sense, then, Etty was no longer defined by what was happening to her; however victimized she was by the external circumstances of her living, she found ways of shaping what her life was about.

Indeed, there is plenty that any of us can do to increase self-responsibility, even in relation to those aspects of our life that relate to being members of marginalized groups. No matter the circumstances, we can always aim for ways to seek and integrate empathy; we can strive to transcend any judgments and enemy images that arise in us; we can cultivate our capacity for empathy even for those who actively harm us or members of our groups. Ultimately, no one can take away from us the power to speak and act from a grounded core within us; to be aware of our needs; to imagine the needs of others; and to take action or make requests that aim to attend to everyone's needs.

And this is why when I engage with people who are themselves from marginalized groups and who are seeking to be on the journey of integrating nonviolence and specifically NVC, this is how I work with them. Doing this work, especially when we have had enormously difficult lives, is a doorway into freedom from any notion that we are determined by our circumstances. It allows us to see the potential for transcendence right up to the brink of existence.

And, in parallel with this, I want to also remember the limits of this approach. As liberating as this path of self-responsibility has been for me and so many others I have worked with over the years, I am profoundly worried about saying that in principle we have the power to shape our inner experience without immediately qualifying it by saying that in practice, our capacity to do this is constrained by the circumstances of our life, most especially by our position in society. Otherwise, I could easily see any of us who is in a position of privilege being seduced by this beauty into not seeing the imbalances in the world, and thus contributing to further marginalization of already marginalized groups.

The first thing I note is that the power of self-responsibility is an accomplishment that requires a bunch of inner work. Access to the resources that make inner work possible is itself mediated by privilege. People from marginalized groups tend to have less access to the resources that make this kind of inner work possible. The obstacle to self-responsibility is higher.

At the very same time that such inner work is made more challenging by social marginalization, the rate of incidents that bombard the life and consciousness of marginalized groups is far, far higher than for those in the dominant groups. In other words: this affects women more than men; global south people more than global north; lower class people more than higher class; darker skinned people more than lighter skinned... and so on across the many crisscrossing lines of division in society.

This usually results in a much larger and continually growing pile of incidents, events, and history to work through to get to full self-responsibility. As hard as it may be to face the truth, it's there: the comfort of a middle class life in a European or North American country, for a lighter skinned person, especially if they are male, heterosexual, and able-bodied, is not the norm. I want to remain forever aware of that.

In short, what we have for marginalized groups is a larger pile with less access to resources to work through any pile. It makes it dangerously easy to believe that people from marginalized groups are not developed enough as individuals instead of seeing the systemic context within which they live. This is why recognizing self-responsibility is not a substitute for calling those of us from positions of privilege to take responsibility in our own ways.

## Receiving Feedback from People with Less Access to Resources

As part of my general commitment to nonviolence, and, specifically, to taking 100% responsibility for every relationship and every interaction, to the best of my ability, I always want to focus on my path and what I can do to support the relationship and the mutual learning rather than on the other person's path and how they can better be on it. Unless someone has made it explicit that they want to receive feedback from me, for example on how they can express themselves more effectively and be heard more easily by others, my focus is on what I can do to hear them; not on telling them what they can do so I can hear them with more ease.

This is all the more critical when someone from a marginalized group is taking the enormous step of offering feedback, including within a community of practice, about how that very community is contributing to the marginalization of that person.

In this context, I want those of us with more resources to be willing to hear the message and to take responsibility for our part without "requiring" so much work from others before we will take their feedback seriously. Otherwise, teachings about self-responsibility, as liberating as they can be in some contexts, can in other contexts become subtle obstacles to full inclusion of people whose lives have been made horrifically more difficult because of the legacy and current applications of patriarchy, colonialism, and capitalism. This becomes even more painfully so given how much trauma any of those systems generates in those affected by it.

Instead of pilling obstacles and in this way reinforcing our privilege, when we receive feedback well we can actually accelerate the capacity of people from marginalized groups to move forward in their inner liberation. Those of us who have more access to resources can, as often as possible, acknowledge differences in access to resources, and take responsibility for our part in contributing to the difficulties in the lives of marginalized groups. A huge part of the heavy weight that people in marginalized groups have is the exhaustion and loneliness of having to do the work alone, without the support, empathy, and mourning of those of us in the groups that have and continue to create and sustain the conditions of difficulty for marginalized groups. Often, we do this even when we are motivated by a desire to contribute to the well-being of the marginalized.

To be more pointed, I have come to believe that any time we ask people from marginalized groups to focus on self-responsibility at the very time when they are taking the enormous risk of speaking truthfully of their experience rather than hiding it, we are reinforcing the very power differences that they are inviting us to look at.

We do this by implicitly asserting that we are the "authority" on how people are supposed to speak before we would hear them. We do this by making what's important to us—how people speak—more important than what's important to the person speaking to us—the content of what they want us to hear. Overall, we render their act of offering feedback impotent, because we distract attention away from taking in the feedback, regardless of form, and from showing that learning and transformation can happen on our end.

## Taking Responsibility from a Position of Privilege

Taking in feedback in full rests, in part, on the capacity to take responsibility for the effect of our actions instead of focusing on being seen for our intentions. Simple conceptually, this rarely happens. Instead, a difficult dynamic frequently takes place. Its steps happen in sequence, are rarely interrupted, and are all too familiar to people in marginalized positions and to some of us who have applied ourselves over years to study the dynamics which would otherwise be invisible to us. I know this because I have been part of this kind of dynamic, more than once, and have subsequently seen it from the outside many times.

- First, someone in a position of privilege does something that subtly or grossly, consciously or unconsciously, reinforces their position of privilege.
- Second, a person in a marginalized position speaks up about it, likely after witnessing many such incidents before, either affecting them or someone else from their group. Perhaps because of years of holding back; perhaps because of many attempts to speak and then not being heard; perhaps because of generalized exhaustion and trauma, the speaking of the feedback is not done with the degree of care, consciousness, skillfulness, self-responsibility, or orientation to vision that, in most circumstances, we might wish.
- Third, the person in the position of privilege reacts to what is being said by becoming upset, expressing a critique about how the feedback is spoken, and/or calling attention to their intentions.
- Fourth, the attention in the group moves to the person in the position of privilege, leaving the person from the marginalized group alone in the very moment they are most in need of support. Most tragically, more often than not, the attention doesn't ever go back to the person who spoke up. The content of their feedback is not addressed. Learning doesn't occur. And the trauma of marginalization increases.

In calling attention to this dynamic, I want to stress that I find it completely clear why the person who is being given feedback wants to focus on intention. Especially because I have been that person, I know that it's excruciatingly difficult to maintain the focus on effect when we so very much want to be seen for our intention. The tragic reality of life in our patriarchal cultures is that extremely few of us have enough of a positive, accepting, warm relationship with ourselves that can serve as an anchor for doing this difficult work.

Because this capacity is both so difficult and so vitally and critically needed to be able to transform our communities of practice, whatever they are, I have committed myself to do two things as my part in creating a shift. One is to continue to do my own work, and the other is to write and teach about what I learn both from my work and from witnessing others' work.

When I manage to enhance my capacity to hear the contents of what people from marginalized groups share about their experiences, regardless of how it's presented, two things happen. One is that I build more solid relationships with people who don't have the specific privileges that I have. This, in itself, already subverts the divide-and-conquer structures that patriarchy continues to create. The second is that, both on my own and together with those whose feedback I made myself available to integrate, the community of practice as a whole becomes more conscious and more unified.

As more of us take this route, first, the community can begin to nurture and strengthen the voices that are willing to speak of marginalization. Then, with enough strength building, the community can come together to look at the effects of power on how we operate, and to mourn those experiences in community. In this way, over time, the group becomes a more conscious community that has the capacity to grapple more effectively with the horrific legacy of patriarchy and its offspring such as capitalism and white supremacy. In the end, everyone is freer.

Before ending, I want to undo any misconception that anything can be done in isolation. I would not possibly be able to reach this point of clarity and willingness to speak, first within the community and now beyond, without active support from colleagues and friends, some from predominantly privileged groups, some from predominantly marginalized groups, and some, like me, sitting uncomfortably in both worlds. We are interdependent creatures. The work of facing and transforming our privilege is nothing short of transforming our delusion of being entirely individual beings, so we can take back our place within the family of life.

> *"If all men are oppressors, then what were they supposed to do? Was there nothing that men could do right? Was I simply advocating for male genocide?"*

# In Confronting Privilege, We Should Focus on Systems and Not Individuals

*Nian Hu*

*In the following viewpoint Nian Hu writes that in calling men and other beneficiaries of privilege oppressors, she is not levelling criticism at particular people. Instead, her focus is on the systems that allow certain members of society to benefit from privilege and others to be oppressed by it. She recognizes that she herself is a privileged member of society and that as such, she is an oppressor of the less privileged. Instead of focusing on individuals, she maintains, we must dismantle the systems that allow the privileged to flourish at the expense of the marginalized. Nian Hu is a journalist and copywriter based in New York. She is a 2018 graduate of Harvard, where she wrote op-eds for the* Harvard Crimson.

"Check Your Privilege," by Nian Hu, The Harvard Crimson, April 6, 2017. Reprinted by permission.

As you read, consider the following questions:

1. Why were many men angered by a previous column that Hu wrote?
2. Why does she not consider her criticism of male privilege a personal attack?
3. How does Hu's own self-criticism in which she identifies herself as a person of privilege aid in furthering her point?

In my last article, I wrote about how men benefit from male privilege. I wrote about how men, on a structural level, benefit from a system that establishes male dominance at the expense of women. I wrote, in no uncertain terms, that men are and will always be oppressors.

These statements proved to be extremely controversial. Men, especially those who consider themselves feminists, were angry that I called them oppressors. They invoked the "not all men" argument, and brought up all the ways in which they have supported women's rights. Many men seemed to consider my statements a personal attack, and became defensive. If all men are oppressors, then what were they supposed to do? Was there nothing that men could do right? Was I simply advocating for male genocide?

This controversy, I believe, stems from a fundamental misunderstanding of what privilege and oppression mean. Privilege is the idea that society grants unearned benefits to people because of certain aspects of their identity. And, on the flip side, there is oppression—the idea that society disadvantages people because of certain aspects of their identity. Privileged people, therefore, benefit at the expense of oppressed people.

However, privilege and oppression need to be understood in the context of larger power structures. Society is affected by different power structures—patriarchy, white supremacy, classism, and ableism, to name only a few. Under these power structures, privileged people hold institutional power over oppressed groups. Under the patriarchy, for example, men are the ones who hold political, economic, and social power. And indeed, if you look around the world, top political and economic leaders are almost all men. Men are overwhelmingly in charge of running companies and corporations, making and adjudicating laws, and producing knowledge.

Privilege, therefore, has nothing to do with individuals, and everything to do with larger power systems and structures in society. The structures in our society that bestow unearned benefits to men are the same ones that oppress women. This does not mean that every single individual man in the world is committing violence against women. It only means that, as long as the structures of patriarchy and sexism exist in the world, men are oppressors who will benefit at the expense of women.

Understandably, nobody likes being called an oppressor. But it is critical to acknowledge all the ways in which you are an oppressor. For example, I am an oppressor. As a cisgender and heterosexual person, I benefit from the oppression of LGBT people. As an able-bodied person, I benefit from the oppression of people with disabilities. The power structures of heterosexism, cissexism, and ableism grant me unearned benefits at the expense of LGBT people and people with disabilities.

But, once again, oppression and privilege are concepts that refer to structures, not individuals. When I say that I am an oppressor, I do not mean that I personally engage in violence against transgender people. I do not mean that I personally design buildings that are inaccessible to people in wheelchairs. In fact, as an individual, I strive to do the opposite. I strive to be an ally to the LGBT and disabled communities, and I acknowledge that I can and should always do more for those communities.

But at the end of the day, I can't stop being an oppressor. No matter how many charities I donate to, how many LGBT rallies I attend, how many articles about ableism I read, or how many Crimson staff editorials about transgender rights I help write—I am still an oppressor. It doesn't matter how well-intentioned I am.

I will still indirectly benefit from the violence that is inflicted on those communities.

When society centers the experiences of heterosexual people as valid—for example, by allowing me to hold hands with my partner in public without fear of harassment and by portraying straight people almost exclusively in the media—it simultaneously marginalizes the experiences of LGBT people as invalid, deviant, and criminal.

When society caters exclusively to able-bodied people such as myself—for example, by designing buildings without ramps or by implementing education systems that prioritize only certain types of learning—it simultaneously oppresses people with disabilities by depriving them of access to education and physical buildings.

And so, it is time for us to move the conversation away from individuals and back towards structures. It is not helpful or productive when members of privileged groups demand recognition for their good deeds, or insist that "not all men" or "not all straight people" or "not all able-bodied people" are bad people. That is not what the conversation is about.

Instead, we need to focus on dismantling the power structures in society. For men, this means actively working to undo the structure of patriarchy. And for myself, this means actively working to undo the structures of heterosexism, cissexism, and ableism. We all have a lot of work to do. But the first step towards a more equitable world is the acknowledgement of our own privilege, and the ways in which we benefit from the oppression of others.

> *"Getting blokes on board is not a magic solution to gender inequality, the report notes, but without it the 'systematic pattern of female disadvantage and male privilege' is unlikely to change quickly."*

# Men Must Be Part of the Solution to Male Privilege

## Catherine Fox

*In the following viewpoint Catherine Fox argues that men need to take the lead in ending male privilege in the work place. But getting men to end a system in which they were the primary beneficiaries is not easy. Many men are reluctant to help and practice passive resistance. Fortunately, there are many executives who are on board with promoting gender equity, and they understand the advantages of a system where both sexes can flourish. Catherine Fox is an Australian journalist, author, feminist, and public speaker. Her books include* Stop Fixing Women: Why Building Fairer Workplaces Is Everybody's Business.

"Getting Men on Board Is Part of the Solution to Female Disadvantage at Work," by Catherine Fox, Guardian News and Media Limited, June 14, 2017. Reprinted by permission.

As you read, consider the following questions:

1. How does the author's introduction about a man who was uncomfortable with "gender" set up the rest of her essay?
2. According to the viewpoint, how will men benefit from gender equity?
3. What are some examples of how men can act to promote gender equity?

A few years ago a well-known chief executive who had recently joined the Male Champions of Change group told me he found the whole "gender area" a bit difficult because he grew up without sisters, went to a boys' school, then studied and worked in a male-dominated field.

He seemed to have forgotten that he'd been raised by a mother and lived in a society made up of nearly 51% women. And that men have a gender too.

Like quite a few of his peers in the group, he was out of his comfort zone and starting to learn some unpleasant realities about his own privilege and what that means for the women who make up nearly 47% of the Australian workforce.

Men are part of the problem and need to be part of the solution, authors Graeme Russell and Michael Flood point out in a timely new Diversity Council Australia report titled *Men Make a Difference: Engaging Men on Gender Equality.*

Getting blokes on board is not a magic solution to gender inequality, the report notes, but without it the "systematic pattern of female disadvantage and male privilege" is unlikely to change quickly. This was also my conclusion in my book, *Stop Fixing Women: Why Building Fairer Workplaces is Everybody's Business* (NewSouth).

Men are key to addressing an uneven system largely sustained by them, the report notes, but not because women are weak or can't contribute. It's about changing how men think, behave and relate to women and other men.

Genuine engagement however involves two uncomfortable home truths about most workplaces: that power needs to be shared but is still largely in the hands of men; and men have traditionally been the beneficiaries of "unearned" benefits.

Men's views are often taken more seriously, they are evaluated more positively and seen as more "natural" leaders. Challenging those biases, my research suggests, needs to start with those at the top who can change the rules and deal with resistance.

It's not about simply turning up to White Ribbon Day or men calling themselves feminists.

In fact, the report makes it clear that effective efforts should avoid putting men on pedestals or hiding behind token efforts—often known as "gender-washing" because there's more talk than action. And male advocacy is not a replacement for—but should sit alongside—programs that support women.

But getting buy-in is still hard work: men don't think it's their problem, they fear judgement by their peers if they speak up, and many claim they don't know what to say or do.

But there's also a major upside, Flood and Russell point out: men will benefit from progress towards gender equality personally, in their intimate and family relationships, and in their workplaces and communities. And most men broadly support gender equality.

In fact, men may even find it easier to make an impact, whether individually or through the Male Champions of Change, programs such as the Workplace Gender Equilibrium Challenge or networks like The 100% Project.

Research shows that because men at the higher levels of workplaces can take for granted their gender and leadership positions and their acceptance by masculine establishments, they are often perceived more positively than women when acting as public champions.

But passive resistance is still rife within many organisations, where the latest diversity measures are often seen as "unfair" to men. Backlash is particularly virulent in the middle ranks of management—sometimes called the concrete layer.

No wonder it's so much easier and less disruptive to tell women they need to "lean in" or gain confidence, which leaves the status quo in place.

The male leaders I interviewed were clear that they had to face up to the reality of what happened in their own workplaces and put their foot down to get new rules embedded.

They did more than talk and were using interventions to prevent bias in recruiting, promoting and paying employees. Examples included anonymous recruiting, which removes candidates' names from applications, reviewing how work was allocated to ensure women were getting similar experience and opportunities to their peers, and conducting pay audits to identify gender gaps.

This included Lance Hockridge, former CEO of Aurizon, who introduced new recruitment programs and targets, and made sure he spoke directly to dissenters; and Martin Parkinson, former treasury secretary (now secretary of the department of prime minister and cabinet) who realised the work done in the past had dealt with symptoms and not the cause of the problem.

Several of these men acknowledged their efforts didn't make them very popular in the ranks, but they were motivated by a strong sense of justice and the upside for their business.

And like the chair of Diversity Council Australia, former Australian of the Year and chief of army, David Morrison, they agreed that once you see sexism you can't unsee it.

Gender equality is a business issue, not a women's issue, concludes the report which provides much-needed research and advice by men on how to engage men in this effort.

Fixing women hasn't delivered fairer outcomes because it only focuses on half the workforce and reinforces the stereotypes that underpin an unequal system.

Now we need the men who designed our workplaces and mostly run them to take action. They are the system and they need to help change it.

> *"Most of the rich people who try to do something about inequality give some of their money away. Yet philanthropy isn't an ideal tool for fixing inequality, as research by economists like Indraneel Dasgupta and Ravi Kanbur has shown."*

# Some Rich People Are Trying to Fix Inequality

## Erynn Beaton

*In the following viewpoint, Erynn Beaton discusses how income inequality is not just unfair but poses an existential threat to democracy. The rich have an outsized influence on government, politics, and society, but there are some wealthy Americans who are trying to do something about inequality. But traditional philanthropy, exemplified by giving one's money away, is not actually the best solution to the problem, Beaton says. Instead, the entire economic system must undergo reform in order to fix the problem. Many wealthy individuals are reluctant to change a system that has worked in their favor, but doing so many be worth it. Erynn Beaton is assistant professor in the John Glenn College of Public Affairs at Ohio State University.*

"How Some Rich People Are Trying to Dismantle Inequality," by Erynn Beaton, The Conversation, 07/21/2017. https://theconversation.com/how-some-rich-people-are-trying-to-dismantle-inequality-80369. Licensed under CC BY-ND 4.0 International.

As you read, consider the following questions:

1. How have some wealthy businesspeople sought to help out their workers?
2. Why are some people ashamed of being rich?
3. Why is philanthropy not the ideal solution for fixing income inequality, according to the viewpoint?

Ample research indicates that the growing problem of wealth and income inequality could stunt U.S. economic growth and undermine our democracy while stirring political polarization. Given that the federal government shows little interest in fighting economic inequality and many states are ill-equipped to do much about it, what else can be done?

Studies have also found that the rich exert far more influence over government than the rest of us. This imbalance means that wealthy people who do something about inequality may have more power to make an impact than everybody else. As scholars of social change, we wanted to learn more about how a small number of affluent Americans choose to spend their own time, clout and money fighting inequality.

## A Growing Gap

The latest official estimates indicate that the richest 10 percent held 76 percent of the nation's wealth as of 2013. That means for every US$10, these Americans own $7.60, leaving $2.40 for the remaining 90 percent. And the concentration of wealth is only getting worse. The richest 10 percent held only 67 percent of the nation's wealth in 1989.

Growing inequality is inspiring some rich people to do something about it by influencing public policy and corporations. For example, Morris Pearl, previously the managing director of investment firm Blackrock, has lobbied to close the carried interest tax loophole, which many financial managers use to significantly lower the income taxes they pay. Hamdi Ulukaya, founder of

Chobani Yogurt, gave his employees an ownership stake in the company prior to its sale, even though he could have made more himself if he had not.

## Looking in the Mirror

Businessman T.J. Zlotnitsky offers another apt example of this demographic. After making a fortune with his tech company, he wants companies to pay higher wages and the government to tax the rich more. Zlotnitsky belongs to Patriotic Millionaires, a group of rich people bent on fighting inequality. As he explained in a blog post:

> My story wouldn't be possible without the uniquely American combination of opportunity and public services that my family was able to tap into.

To learn more about people like him, we conducted interviews with 20 people who live across the country and belong to a nonprofit organization dedicated to creating a more fair economy. (We agreed not to name it.) All of the people we spoke with consider themselves to be "wealthy allies" who work alongside people of much more modest means to reduce economic inequality. These rich people epitomized wealth in America: most were white men. They spanned all ages. Some had inherited their fortune, while others were raised in households with modest means and made their wealth over the course of their careers.

Like Zlotnitsky, most wealthy people fighting inequality who we spoke with told us they had gone through a reflective process to recognize the advantages their status has afforded them while getting involved in this effort.

First, they accepted that they partly owed their wealth to a system that works in their favor and not merely to their own merits and efforts. Realizing that they owe their wealth partially to systematic advantages and luck was challenging because it requires overcoming the popular belief that people get what they deserve. Chuck Collins, who inherited and gave away his share of the Oscar

## Privilege Has a Price

What is our responsibility concerning the oppression that exists as a result of our inherent privilege? I'm all for people taking personal responsibility in their lives. However privilege has a price. Part of the price is the responsibility to challenge our privilege, work towards dismantling it and becoming allies to those who pay the cost of it via oppression. There is no privilege without oppression. There is no justice without hard work. I'm not talking about the hard work we bought into when we were handed the American Dream at birth. Instead, I'm talking about actual hard work. The kind that requires us to break our dysfunctional loyalty towards our inherent privilege. Here, briefly, is what that hard work looks like:

- Reflecting on our own privilege and the impact it has on folks who fall outside of such privilege. In other words, flip the script and see how circumstances change when you view the world through a different lens. If you were born being marginalized by a culture that validates those who are privileged, what might the world look like for you?
- Becoming allies, comrades and human shields to those whom our privilege brings constant suffering. Men become allies for women,

Mayer fortune, told a tale of self-awareness in a memoir he called "Born on Third Base." Collins now advocates for preserving the estate tax and does research on inequality to bring more attention to the issue.

The next step is overcoming shame. Acknowledging their privilege made many of the people we interviewed feel ashamed. For example, a bisexual woman who inherited nearly $1 million on her 21st birthday said she found it harder to come out to her friends as wealthy than as a lesbian. Hearing over and over that identifying as rich was disconcerting surprised us because many Americans claim their wealth as evidence of merit.

In addition to overcoming their guilt and shame, wealthy allies often fear the ire of other rich people. Their peers got mad at them

males for females, white folks for people of color, heterosexuals for the LBGTQ community, humans towards all other species.
- Listening to folks and believing their circumstances.
- Following instead of leading when it comes to supporting folks fighting for justice.
- Committing treason against privilege and therefore loyalty towards justice.

If we continue to take the same action we've always taken then we can expect the same results. Those with privilege have always believed they weren't part of the problem. One will quickly come to realize that the version of hard work we've been handed is quite easy in comparison to the real hard work most of us, I dare say, have not yet begun; challenging our own privilege in the pursuit of true justice for all of us. Applying these guidelines will most likely be the hardest, most difficult work of our lives. Why? Simply because they require us to take responsibility and make the necessary changes in order to find a life we're unfamiliar with … one full of empathy.

"What Is Your Responsibility as a Person of Privilege?" by Mike Sliwa, Good Men Project.com, 07/24/2016. https://goodmenproject.com/featured-content/responsibility-person-privilege-wcz/.

for doing things that arguably violate their own economic interests, such as advocating for taxes targeting the rich.

The people we interviewed all said they consider these challenges hard but necessary parts of the process of becoming a wealthy ally. Many said they relied on people like themselves for moral support.

## The Limits of Philanthropy

Most of the rich people who try to do something about inequality give some of their money away. Yet philanthropy isn't an ideal tool for fixing inequality, as research by economists like Indraneel Dasgupta and Ravi Kanbur has shown.

The rich people we interviewed who wanted to side with the poor seemed to think about philanthropy differently than their peers. All donated at least some of their wealth, and some have given their entire fortunes away. But most of them also tried to go further by lobbying Congress to raise taxes on the rich or urging corporate boards to raise worker pay—two potential ways to reduce inequality.

Some of the people we interviewed said they believed that they had found another path to make their philanthropy more effective. For example, one man admitted to himself that he might not be the best person to determine where his money should be spent. After years of giving money to charities started and run by upper-middle-class men like himself, he began giving to organizations that were started and led by the poor. In this way, he handed over his elite power to the poor, trusting that they knew better how to raise themselves up than he did.

As this example demonstrates, acting as a wealthy ally to dismantle economic inequality requires a paradigm shift. Wealthy allies said they believed that the most effective way for them to fight inequality is by willingly handing over their power to the poor. This shift can make it uncomfortable for rich people to join the movement to fight inequality. But if their efforts help preserve our democracy and our economy, it may be worth it.

"*I am not against discussion, but we aren't going to talk our way out of this. I am not against education, but we aren't going to train our way out of this. What I am for is action.*"

# Enough Talk, Let's Act to Improve Society

## Iain De Jong

*In the following viewpoint, Iain De Jong provides a rousing response to centuries of inaction that have allowed unequal systems to persist in countries such as the United States, Canada, and Australia. As he points out the many inequities, he also states that doing so is no answer. The only answers to systemic systems of privilege are in action, thus De Jong is working actively along with others to change the system where some flourish and many others are left behind. In order to help solve problems money is a necessity, and all privileged people should pay their fair share of taxes. Iain De Jong is president and CEO of OrgCode, a consulting firm dedicated to ending homelessness in developed countries around the world.*

"White Privilege and Housing and Homelessness," by Iain De Jong, OrgCode Consulting, November 26, 2014. Reprinted by permission.

As you read, consider the following questions:

1. What significance is there to the author's mentioning that he was in St. Louis "last week"?
2. What examples does the author use to show the disparity between whites and blacks?
3. How are lower taxes an example of white privilege in action?


Last week I was in St. Louis. The tension was palpable. It was a community on edge, awaiting the grand jury decision regarding Officer Wilson in the shooting of Michael Brown. This week, with the decision in Ferguson making world headlines, the result has been many talking about reforms, righting injustices, addressing inequities, making adjustments in society so that complex social issues that involve race are considered differently.

Legacies of injustice continue. In the United States it is the painful history of slavery and the treatment of African-Americans and maltreatment of Native Americans too. (A "civilized" nation that celebrates Columbus Day?) In Canada and Australia it is the painful history of colonization of indigenous peoples and failed, unjust attempts at assimilation through the likes of residential schools. (In Canada there is still something called the Indian Act— legislation that governs engagement between the state and what is allowed for a group of people, to put it over-simply).

If you are not white, you are disproportionately going to be represented in a homeless population in the United States, Canada and Australia. This isn't a coincidence.

If you are not white, you are less likely to be a homeowner. You are less likely to have financial assistance from family to purchase into the homeownership market. If you are not white you are less likely to meet financial risk assessment thresholds to purchase a home. If you are not white and you do own a home, the value of your home is, on average, less than that of a white person. This isn't a coincidence.

If you are not white, you will be incarcerated at a disproportionately higher rate. The biggest investment made in housing is the "big house". This is not a coincidence.

If you are not white, you are less likely to get appropriate mental health assistance or assistance with a substance use disorder. This is not a coincidence.

If you are not white, you are more likely to make less money than white counterparts, unless you are working in a unionized environment. If you are not white, you are more likely to not be in a management position. This is not a coincidence.

If you are not white, you are less likely to finish high school and less likely to complete a post high school degree. This is not a coincidence.

Did I—a white, educated, straight, male—make more not white people homeless or decrease their homeownership rates or incarcerate people in a disproportionate manner, deprive others of mental health assistance or substance use recovery, pay an unequal wage or decrease educational attainment of people that are not white? No. But that doesn't mean I am not part of the problem.

If I want to be part of the solution, I have to acknowledge that I am definitely part of the problem. Try as I might, my white privilege makes it impossible for me to truly empathize beyond a cerebral exercise in our current society because the likelihood of success is stacked heavily in my favor. I didn't ask for any of this. It is a privilege bestowed upon me solely by being white, and I will never know what it is like to be not white. Do I give up in trying to understand wholeheartedly? No.

I need an education different than what multiple university degrees have provided me. I need to ensure that all I do is rooted firmly in the tenets of justice, and not one of pity or sympathy or charity. I need to speak truth to power and talk about the thing that others sometimes don't want to talk about, beyond just "Have you noticed that most of the people in your shelter are African-American?" (or aboriginal) to "What are we going to do about the disproportionate number of African-American (or aboriginal) people needing housing?"

When I have half-heartedly attempted these discussions in the past it is usually met with responses like, "It took generations to get to the point where things are this bad, and it is going to take generations to get out of this situation." Or, "I know bad things happened in the past. I didn't do it. It wasn't my fault. When are they going to get over it?" Or, "The problem is that they don't have fathers in their life or role models to set them straight on how to make a living and take care of themselves." Or, "I almost feel better for them when they are incarcerated, because at least then you know they are getting fed and access to health care." Or, "You know it's because they really can't handle alcohol." Or, "They've never had an apartment because of how their people are. We are just setting them up for failure." Or, "Of course there are more of them homeless"—as if all of these statements normalize reality so that no action can be taken—and are accepted on face value as truths.

I will take these inflammatory comments head on from now on in all situations.

See, these aren't African-American problems. They are American problems. These aren't Native Canadian problems. They are Canadian problems. These aren't Indigenous Australian problems. They are Australian problems. It isn't someone else's problem. It is our collective problem.

I am not against discussion, but we aren't going to talk our way out of this. I am not against education, but we aren't going to train our way out of this. What I am for is action.

I have said many times that it is pointless to gather race or ethnic data if you aren't going to do anything with it—if it is just an academic exercise or to gather descriptive data then it is pointless. Maybe it is time that we find the point and act on the point.

Economic injustice and racism are siblings…perhaps even twins. I am opposed to anti-poverty strategies. I am all for increased wealth strategies. I will not pity people for their poverty. I will not advocate just to increase benefit rates. I will rally against why it exists in the first place.

I will work to reform any system that calls itself a "justice system" when it systemically removes people's access to employment and housing, and does so in many instances for a lifetime. If we can't agree that time served is, um, time served—then maybe we need to start calling it the racially unjust punishment system.

I will advocate that we intentionally work to decrease stigma of mental illness and substance addiction with people of color. I will no longer accept the narrative of "it's cultural" thrown around by white people in avoiding getting people the assistance they deserve.

And one more thing.

I will never vote for the candidate wanting to lower my taxes. Why? Because this is the manifestation of white privilege at its finest. We can't have less money in the coffers of government and expect more or better interventions to address these systemic and systematic issues. Lowering taxes will not decrease homelessness. Lowering taxes will not increase available housing. Lowering taxes will not result in better education. Lowering taxes will not improve human services. A vote for the candidate wanting to lower taxes—who will give you the mantra of better service at less cost or efficiencies as propaganda—is a vote for ongoing injustice, more racial inequity, and more white privilege.

> *"Affirmative action is an important*
> *counterweight against such privilege*
> *and elitism and helps to promote*
> *the inclusion of diverse voices—*
> *particularly of women, people*
> *of color, and other marginalized*
> *groups—in universities, workplaces,*
> *and other societal institutions."*

# Affirmative Action Functions as a Counterweight to Privilege

*Betty Hung*

*In the following viewpoint, Betty Hung uses Brett Kavanaugh's confirmation to the US Supreme Court as a springboard for her argument supporting the virtues of affirmative action. She believes that conservative forces are using Asian Americans as a way to undermine affirmative action, when she herself has benefited from the policy. For Hung, affirmative action functions as a way to counter privilege and allow for a diverse, multicultural leadership in the United States. The alternative is the continued dominance of privileged white affluent males represented by Kavanaugh. The battle over affirmative action is for her a key cultural and political moment as the United States decides what type of nation it wants to be going forward. Betty Hung is a civil rights attorney and an educator.*

"Affirmative Action as Counterweight to Privilege and Elitism," by Betty Hung, edited by Dick Price and Sharon Kyle, October 9, 2018. Reprinted by permission.

As you read, consider the following questions:

1. How is the author's Asian ethnicity important to her argument?
2. How did the author benefit from affirmative action herself?
3. According to Hung, how is our nation at a crossroads regarding power and privilege?

The naked and brutal exercise of power by Republicans in the battle to confirm Brett Kavanaugh to the Supreme Court is a travesty, but unfortunately not surprising. With the rise of the #MeToo movement and demographic shifts that will lead to white people being a minority in the United States by 2045, I believe we are witnessing an effort by privileged white men to hold on to and consolidate their power and control, even if it results in the erosion of our democratic institutions.

One of the key battlegrounds in this power struggle is affirmative action. Since the early 1960s, affirmative action has helped to level the playing field and open doors for women and people of color, providing a tool to address the pervasive gender and racial disparities in our society that continue to limit access to equal opportunity. Yet, affirmative action is under vigorous attack and potentially could be eliminated at universities across the nation.

Harvard is the target of a lawsuit brought by Edward Blum, an anti-civil rights crusader who is using Asian Americans as cover for his efforts to prohibit universities from considering race as one of many factors in the admissions process. The Harvard case is scheduled for federal trial in one week and is anticipated to go up to the Supreme Court. The Trump administration also recently opened federal investigations into allegations that Harvard and Yale discriminate against Asian American applicants.

As we head into an epic battle over affirmative action in university admissions, it is crucial that people who opposed

Kavanaugh's confirmation understand why they also have a stake in the affirmative action fight. A key lesson from the Kavanaugh confirmation process is that it matters who is in positions of power and their life experiences and world view. It mattered that all the Republican members of the Senate Judiciary Committee are white men willing to blatantly disregard survivors and to preserve patriarchy. Affirmative action is an important counterweight against such privilege and elitism and helps to promote the inclusion of diverse voices—particularly of women, people of color, and other marginalized groups—in universities, workplaces, and other societal institutions.

As an Asian American woman, I refuse to be used by conservatives who are trying to exploit Asian Americans as a wedge in their efforts to abolish affirmative action in university admissions. Contrary to the contentions of Blum that affirmative action discriminates against Asian Americans, holistic review that considers race as one of many factors benefits people of all backgrounds, including Asian Americans.

First, affirmative action is shorthand for inclusive admissions policies that consider race and gender, among many factors, allowing for a more holistic assessment of an applicant's life experiences and potential. This results in more diverse student bodies with myriad backgrounds and perspectives which, as demonstrated by the Kavanaugh confirmation battle, is critical given that educational institutions serve as a pipeline to leadership positions that have real life impact on millions of Americans. Especially considering that legacy applicants have a significant advantage in the admissions process—with legacy applicants nearly six times more likely to be admitted at Harvard than non-legacy applicants—affirmative action is necessary to promote equal opportunity for students who are not from backgrounds of privilege and wealth.

Second, affirmative action promotes more diverse educational institutions that better prepare students to develop into stronger and more empathetic leaders who can understand and work with people of wide ranging backgrounds. This is especially critical given the increasingly diverse composition of our communities. California already is majority people of color and the nation will soon follow. In the 2016 Fisher case, in which Blum unsuccessfully challenged affirmative action at the University of Texas, the Supreme Court affirmed the educational benefits of diversity as a compelling interest in upholding the constitutionality of race conscious admissions policies.

My own experience illustrates the positive personal and societal impact of affirmative action—including for Asian Americans.

Affirmative action opened doors for me to Harvard College and Yale Law School in the 1990s. I graduated from a public high school where students rarely were admitted to the Ivy League. If Harvard and Yale Law had considered only grades and test scores, I would not have gotten in. But I was admitted because Harvard and Yale utilized holistic admissions processes that assessed me as a whole person, as more than just my grades and test scores. They also were allowed under the law to consider how race, among many other factors, shaped my life experiences and potential.

Growing up in the San Gabriel Valley, a suburb east of Los Angeles, my family was one of the first Asian families to move into a primarily white and Chicano community that now has the highest concentration of Asian Americans and Latinos anywhere in the nation. Due to an influx of Asian immigrants, including many members of my extended family, there was a nativist backlash in the 1980s. I remember neighbors making fun of my family for speaking Taiwanese and the parents of a white girl who lived a few doors down the block telling her that I was not allowed in their house. When I was in high school, a local mayor, buoyed by vocal anti-immigrant supporters, advocated for a one-year moratorium on immigration and attempted to make English the city's official language.

If race conscious admissions had been prohibited, as Blum desires, Harvard and Yale Law would not have been legally permitted to consider these formative aspects of my life relating to my racial identity and racial experiences—the foundation of

# Is Affirmative Action Racist?

Affirmative action favors non-whites on the faulty assumption that every white person is well-off, and every person of color is poor. Empirical findings from the Hoover Institution support the claim that this policy around the world actually helps upper- and middle-class students from minority backgrounds rather than the less fortunate. This neither aids the disadvantaged towards whom affirmative action was intended, nor equally favors the applications of poor white applicants. To truly even the playing field, admissions preferences should be given on the basis of disadvantage—not on the basis of race.

Not all minorities are protected under affirmative action; in fact, some are actually negatively impacted from of it. A study from Princeton University found that, due to universities' racially based acceptance policies, Asians have an automatic disadvantage in comparison to other students that is equivalent to a loss of 50 SAT points. Not only are Asians required to have higher scores than other minority candidates, but they also need to outperform whites at an equivalent academic level to get accepted to schools. This undermines the efficacy of the SAT as a tool by which to evaluate candidates for acceptance. It also goes against the logic of what affirmative action is trying to do. Additionally, unlike whites, Asians haven't been past victimizers of blacks and Hispanics, and so the compensation-for-past-abuses argument is null and void. With affirmative action, Asians are unduly discriminated against.

While affirmative action was intended to help those with a history of suffering prejudice, racial discrimination isn't properly rectified when favoring one group (minorities) over another (whites). In fact, biased selection policies may fuel resentment and stigmatization towards minorities from those who believe they hold position in the workplace or university due to policy rather than merit. Theories that there is a correlation between intelligence and skin color have been debunked, rendering affirmative action programs more of an insult to underprivileged groups than an asset.

"Is Affirmative Action a Racist Policy?" by Kira Goldring, Perspective Media.

why I wanted to be a civil rights lawyer and that became the focus of my academic studies.

The diverse learning environments at Harvard and Yale were life changing. I learned even more outside the classroom than I did in the classroom. I became friends with people different from me in terms of race, ethnicity, socioeconomic background, geography, religion, and sexual orientation. My rooming group at Harvard included African Americans, Latinas, Whites, and Asian Americans from a wide range of socioeconomic backgrounds. We celebrated our lifelong friendships at our 25th year reunion just a few months ago. Being in community with such diverse people prepared me for a career as a civil rights lawyer working in multiracial, intersectional coalitions. I can trace my ability to work with people across lines of difference back to my time in college and law school.

If we are to lean into—rather than reject—the demographic diversity of the 21st century while upholding principles of inclusion and equity, it is imperative that we preserve and strengthen holistic admissions policies that consider how race, among many factors, shapes an applicant's life experiences. If universities are prohibited from taking into account race, despite the pervasive racial inequities in our society that profoundly impact the lived experiences of people of color, we could witness across the nation a decrease in the racial and ethnic diversity of university campuses, as we have in California after the passage of Proposition 209 in 1996. Less racially diverse campuses would result in less diverse leaders and less diverse leadership bodies— eroding trust in our democratic institutions and potentially in our democracy itself.

Our nation is at a crossroads: will the arc of U.S. democracy bend towards an increasingly equitable and diverse multiracial society or further entrench power and resources primarily in the hands of a privileged white male minority? In the wake of the Kavanaugh confirmation debacle, we need diverse leaders who are rooted in and represent our multiracial, intersectional communities and who are genuinely committed to promoting the general welfare of everyone in our society—not just the privileged and elite.

> "The goal of activism is not to take
> privileges away from those who have
> them, but to extend rights to those
> who are denied them."

# We Need Less Talk and More Action Regarding Privilege

*Mirah Curzer*

*In the following viewpoint, Mirah Curzer suggests that merely talking about privilege is not enough to effect needed change with regard to how society treats its more vulnerable members. The idea of checking one's privilege was a good step in acknowledging that not everyone benefits from equal social status, but words alone are not sufficient to address social inequities. Activism is more important. The so-called privileges that many in our society are denied are actually rights. Calling them privileges does not take into account that basic rights are being denied to many people. No one is asking for the privileged to become less privileged, Curzer asserts. What is needed is for everyone to gain equal status in the workplace, in the streets, and in the eyes of the police. As a society we must work actively "to safeguard the rights of all individuals and groups." Mirah Curzer is an attorney, a feminist, and a photographer. Her articles appear in Medium, the Hill, and the Huffington Post, as well as other publications. She serves as co-chair of the New York City Bar Association's Sex and Law Committee. She lives in Brooklyn, New York.*

"Let's Stop Talking So Much About Privilege," by Mirah Curzer, Medium.com, February 7, 2016. Reprinted by permission.

As you read, consider the following questions:

1. According the viewpoint, why is "the discourse of privilege" inadequate to rectify the inequalities in society?
2. What does the author mean when she states that talking about who has more privilege is "not a contest?"
3. How does the author distinguish between "privileges" and "rights" in this article? What is her point in doing so?

A cknowledging your own privilege or encouraging others to check theirs can be a great starting point for conversation and vehicle for consciousness-raising. But when it comes to meaningful social change, it is not close to enough.

It is not enough to pay lip service to the idea that you are privileged and others are not, and then go about your privileged life ignoring those who lack the basic rights you take for granted. "I acknowledge my privilege" is the new "I'm not a racist, but." It lets people go through the verbal motions and feel virtuous, even if they are not just unhelpful but actually part of the problem.

We need to talk in the language of rights, not privileges, if we want to make any systemic change.

"Check your privilege" started out as a reminder that not everyone's lived experience is the same. It is a way of ensuring that a diversity of perspectives is represented in dialogue. As Sam Dylan Finch at Everyday Feminism explains:

> When someone asks you to 'check your privilege,' what they're really asking you to do is to reflect on the ways that your social status might have given you an advantage—even if you didn't ask for it or earn it—while their social status might have given them a disadvantage.
>
> I have no problem with privilege-checking in the context of academic discourse or social justice debate. It is useful a way of opening someone's eyes to a perspective they might be missing because they have never experienced a certain kind of discrimination or disadvantage.

Where I think the problem lies is in extending the discourse of privilege from theory to action. Activism aims to change the status quo, to make the world better. And yes, it is perfectly true that eradicating racism and sexism and homophobia would also get rid of white privilege and male privilege and straight privilege. But that way of looking at things puts the emphasis in the wrong place.

The goal of activism is not to take privileges away from those who have them, but to extend rights to those who are denied them.

The discourse of privilege is problematic because it demands too little in the context of activism. The issue that needs to be addressed is not that those on top do not understand how much better they have it. A little knowledge and self-awareness is not enough to fix the world. The problem is that there are some groups of people who have been systematically denied their fundamental rights.

Language matters, and a "privilege" is, among other things, the opposite of a right. (As in, students don't have a right to participate in this extracurricular activity, and if they misbehave that privilege will be taken away.)

But the things activists mean when we talk about privilege are not like that—they are rights. The right to be equal pay, the right to bodily autonomy, the right to a presumption of innocence, the right to police protection.

Calling these things privileges instead of rights does not take seriously enough what is being denied to people who lack them.

Another colloquial meaning of "privilege" that makes it a difficult way to talk about injustice is the idea of living a privileged life, as synonymous with a life of luxury. I see this all the time—a person of color tells a white person he has white privilege, and he responds by saying that he's not privileged because he's poor. And they're both right.

Obviously, a poor white man has privilege in that he reaps the benefits of being white and male—like not being stopped by the police for innocent behavior like black men and not living in fear of sexual violence like women. But at the same time, he is not living a "privileged life," because he is working two jobs to make his rent payments and can't afford proper health care. Although he has the privileges of whiteness and maleness, he lacks other privileges like those of wealth.

The discourse of privilege creates false dichotomies and unnecessary tension among people who actually agree with each other. If, instead of demanding that the poor white man must acknowledge his privilege, we remind him that other people are being denied their fundamental rights, he may wholeheartedly agree and eagerly join the movement.

I once had a long discussion with a friend about who had more privilege—a white woman or a black man. We never did come to a resolution, because we were dealing with a fundamental incommensurability of goods (or bads). But really, who cares who has more privilege? It's not a contest. What black men and white women have in common is that each group is denied a set of fundamental rights. They are denied different sub-sets of rights, but both groups are entitled to the full set.

Focusing on privilege makes those who have more rights feel guilty for the rights they enjoy (or angry and defensive at being made to feel guilty). But the guilt of the privileged is not only insufficient to create change, it is actively a bad thing. Everyone has the right to be heard, the right to be considered beautiful, the right not to live in fear.

We should be angry that some people are denied those basic human rights, but no one should ever feel guilty for having them.

Of course, many of the things that get referred to as privilege are not actually rights, but unfair advantages that would cease to exist in a just society. For example, the privilege of being the only voice taken seriously in a conversation, the privilege of being elevated over job applicants of other races or genders, the privilege of having your culture be the dominant one. Those things are not fundamental rights—they are the flip side of oppression. Encouraging people to recognize those privileges makes sense, because it is another way of pointing out oppression. And the recognition of enjoying a privilege of that sort should lead to a certain amount of guilt, and more importantly, a corresponding drive to eradicate such unfair advantages.

But I think the distinction between these unfair privileges and actual rights has gotten muddled, to the detriment of protecting the rights of the persecuted.

The discourse of privilege is originally and fundamentally about education—teaching people to see the world from perspectives other than their own. That's wonderful, but it also has its limits.

We need to hold people accountable for their actions, and not only for failing to recognize their privilege.

Men who objectify women or minimize sexual assault are not just in possession of male privilege—they are sexists. White people who mock black culture or justify police brutality are not just privileged white people—they are racists.

The discourse of privilege fails to hold these people fully accountable for their actions. We shouldn't be waving off racism and sexism and homophobia and other prejudices as mere failures to acknowledge privilege.

We need to demand more. Not just that people understand their privilege, but that they stop perpetuating the violation of other people's rights. Not just that powerful institutions acknowledge non-privileged perspectives, but that they safeguard the rights of all individuals and groups.

We don't want a world with less privilege—we want a world with more rights.

# Periodical and Internet Sources Bibliography

*The following articles have been selected to supplement the diverse views presented in this chapter.*

Rachel Anspach, "Why White People Have a Responsibility to Fight White Supremacy." Dec. 28, 2017. https://www.complex.com/life/2017/12/white-people-create-and-maintain-the-status-quo-so-it-is-up-to-us-to-change-the-status-quo/

Crystal Ayres, "15 Advantages and Disadvantages of Affirmative Action in the Workplace." Nov. 22, 2018. 15-advantages-and-disadvantages-of-affirmative-action-in-the-workplace

Katherine Craig, "My fellow white people: if you're not part of the solution, you're part of the problem." *Guardian.* Sept. 6. 2017. https://www.theguardian.com/commentisfree/2017/sep/06/white-people-solution-problem-munroe-bergdorf-racist

Vikram Dodd, "Police leader calls for laws to allow positive race discrimination." *Guardian.* Feb. 22, 2019. https://www.theguardian.com/uk-news/2019/feb/22/police-leader-calls-for-laws-to-allow-positive-race-discrimination

Gina M. Florio, "6 Ways To Stop White Privilege When You See It." *Bustle.* Dec 30, 2015. https://www.bustle.com/articles/130456-6-ways-to-stop-white-privilege-when-you-see-it

Ryan Honeyman, "White People: Let's Talk About White Supremacy." LIFT Economy. Oct. 24, 2018. https://www.lifteconomy.com/blog/2018/10/24/white-people-lets-talk-about-white-supremacy

David Marcus, "A Conservative Defense of Privilege Theory." *Weekly Standard.* November 6, 2017. https://www.weeklystandard.com/david-marcus/a-conservative-defense-of-privilege-theory

Wiley Reading, "5 Valuable Ways to Use Your White Privilege to Fight Anti-Black Racism." Everyday Feminism. January 21, 2015. https://everydayfeminism.com/2015/01/using-white-privilege-fight-racism/

Jamie Utt, "So, You Think Affirmative Action Gives White People a Disadvantage?" Good Men Project. Sept. 13, 2017. https://goodmenproject.com/featured-content/white-students-disadvantaged-affirmative-action-hesaid/

John Warner, "Affirmative Action for Rich White Kids." Oct. 24, 2018. https://www.insidehighered.com/blogs/just-visiting/affirmative-action-rich-white-kids

Mike Wilner, "Acknowledging Privilege to Tackle Inequality." Medium. Dec. 17, 2014. https://medium.com/@mwil20/acknowledging-privilege-to-tackle-inequality-65b1fd00b52a

John Yoo and James C. Phillips, "An End to Racial Preferences at Last?" *National Review.* Dec. 4, 2018. https://www.nationalreview.com/2018/12/supreme-court-racial-preferences-affirmative-action/

# For Further Discussion

## Chapter 1

1. According to the essays in this chapter, why is it so difficult for those in positions of power to accept their privilege?
2. Many privileged people commonly claim that society is a meritocracy, where those who possess the most ability rise to the top. How does privilege theory undermine this concept, according to the essays in this chapter?
3. Why is the "privilege check" controversial? In your opinion, does it squelch dialogue or raise awareness?

## Chapter 2

1. Are the privileges we may enjoy, often without realizing it, important to recognize or are they trivial and unworthy of notice? How do other authors in this chapter feel about such advantages?
2. Is white privilege a fallacy? Why or why not? How might the concept of privilege be misinterpreted?
3. Is the Black Lives Matter movement valid? Use the viewpoints in this chapter to form your argument.

## Chapter 3

1. Consider the concept of "performative allyship," where men pretend to be allied with the women's movement. Can you find examples of this dynamic in viewpoints and in contemporary society?
2. Is there a glass ceiling, or is that an excuse made by women who can't get ahead in the workplace? Consider the viewpoints in this chapter when building your argument.
3. As women continue to challenge men regarding male privilege, what types of backlash have hindered their progress?

# Chapter 4

1. How can we make sure that people do not overreact when they are called out regarding their privilege? Can you think of practical reasons, having read the viewpoints in this chapter?
2. Do you believe that the privileged in society must be part of the solution? Where in this chapter's viewpoints and in life have privileged individuals been willing to cede power and where haven't they?
3. Which of the strategies outlined in this chapter's viewpoints have the most likelihood of effecting positive and lasting change? Which do not?

# Organizations to Contact

*The editors have compiled the following list of organizations concerned with the issues debated in this book. The descriptions are derived from materials provided by the organizations. All have publications or information available for interested readers. The list was compiled on the date of publication of the present volume; the information provided here may change. Be aware that many organizations take several weeks or longer to respond to inquiries, so allow as much time as possible.*

## American Association of University Women (AAUW)

1310 L Street NW, Suite 1000
Washington, DC 20005
(202)785-7700
email: connect@aauw.org
website: www.aauw.org

The American Association of University Women (AAUW) is a leading voice in promoting equity and education for women and girls. Founded in 1881, AAUW examines and takes positions on important issues—educational, social, economic, and political. Their website includes information on Title IX, Education, Civil Rights, and Economic Equity. A recent article on the site is titled "I Am Worth More: Zoe Spencer on Fighting Racism and Sexism in Academia."

## American Civil Liberties Union (ACLU)

125 Broad Street
New York, NY 10004-2400
(212)549-2500
website: www.aclu.org

The ACLU considers itself to be the nation's guardian of liberty, working in courts, legislatures, and communities to defend and preserve the individual rights and liberties that the Constitution and the laws of the United States guarantee. Among the issues they focus on are human rights, racial equality, and women's rights.

Recent articles on their blog include "Saturday Night Live's Sasheer Zamata: Let's Talk About Privilege," and "Black Lives Matter in Our Courtrooms Too."

## American Enterprise Institute for Public Policy Research (AEI)

American Enterprise Institute
1789 Massachusetts Avenue NW
Washington, DC 20036
(202)862-5800
email: tyler.castle@aei.org
website: www.aei.org

The American Enterprise Institute is a conservative public policy think tank that sponsors original research on the world economy, US foreign policy and international security, and domestic political and social issues. AEI is dedicated to defending human dignity, expanding human potential, and building a freer and safer world. Their scholars and staff advance ideas rooted in their belief in democracy and free enterprise.

## Cato Institute

1000 Massachusetts Avenue NW
Washington, D.C. 20001-5403
(202) 842-0200
website: www.cato.org

The Cato Institute is a libertarian public policy research organization, a think tank dedicated to the principles of individual liberty, limited government, free markets, and peace. Its scholars and analysts conduct independent research on a wide range of policy issues. Recent articles include "Gun Privilege in Black and White" and "Value and Opportunity: The Issue of Comparable Pay for Comparable Worth."

## Center for American Progress

1333 H Street NW, 10th Floor
Washington, DC 20005
(202) 682-1611
website: www.americanprogress.org

The Center for American Progress is a public policy research and advocacy organization which presents a liberal viewpoint on economic and social issues. Their website includes a range of articles on various forms of privilege, including "Examining White Privilege," "Confronting White Privilege," "The Conundrum of White-Male Privilege," and "Male Privilege and the Birth Control Debate."

## David Horowitz Freedom Center (formerly the Center for the Study of Popular Culture)

P.O.Box 55089
Sherman Oaks, CA 91499-1964
(800) 752-6562
website: www.horowitzfreedomcenter.org

The center was founded in 1988 by political activist David Horowitz and Peter Collier. It runs several websites and blogs, including *FrontPage Magazine,* Students for Academic Freedom, and Jihad Watch.

## Feminist Majority Foundation (FMF)

East Coast Office
1600 Wilson Boulevard, Suite 801
Arlington, VA 22209
(703) 522-2214
West Coast Office (Los Angeles, CA)
433 S. Beverly Drive
Beverly Hills, CA 90212
(310)556-2500
email: media@feminist.org
website: www.feminist.org

The origin of the Feminist Majority Foundation was inspired by a Newsweek/Gallup public opinion poll that showed the majority of women (56 percent) in the United States self-identified as feminists. Their research and action programs focus on advancing the legal, social, and political equality of women with men; countering the backlash against women's rights; and recruiting and training young feminists to encourage future leadership for the feminist movement in the United States. Their website contains numerous publications related to women's causes.

## National Organization for Women (NOW)

1100 H Street NW, 3rd Floor
Washington, DC 20005
(202) 628-8669
email: www.now.org/about/contact-us/
website: www.now.org

The National Organization for Women considers itself to be the grassroots arm of the women's movement and is dedicated to its multi-issue and multi-strategy approach to women's rights. NOW has hundreds of chapters and hundreds of thousands of members and activists in all fifty states and the District of ColumbiaNOW's purpose is to take action to promote feminist ideals, lead societal change, eliminate discrimination, and achieve and protect the equal rights of all women and girls in all aspects of social, political, and economic life. Articles on its website include "Challenges Faced by African-American Girls Deserve Equal Attention" and "Congress Must Pass the Paycheck Fairness Act and Stop the Theft of Women's Wages."

## National Urban League

80 Pine Street, 9th Floor
New York, NY 10005
(212)558-5300
email: nul.iamempowered.com/contact-us
website: www.nul.org

The Urban League movement strives to enable African Americans and other underserved urban residents to secure economic self-reliance, parity, power and civil rights. The organization focuses on four initiatives that empower urban communities: education, employment, housing, and healthcare. Their publications, available through their website, include *State of Black America* and *Diversity Studies.*

## National Women's Law Center (NWLC)

11 Dupont Circle NW, #800
Washington, DC 20036
(202) 588 5180
website: www. nwic.org

The National Women's Law Center fights for gender justice in court, in public policy, and in society. They focus on issues that are central to the lives of women and girls. The use legal means to change culture and drive solutions to the gender inequity that shapes our society and to break down barriers. They especially aid those who face multiple forms of discrimination, including women of color, LGBQ people, and low-income women and families. Their website includes writings on racial inequality, women's issues, gender equity, and the time's up movement.

## US Commission on Civil Rights (USCCR)

U.S. Commission on Civil Rights
1331 Pennsylvania Avenue, NW, Suite 1150
Washington, DC 20425
(202) 376-7700
website: www.usccr.gov

Established as an independent, bipartisan, fact-finding govenment agency, the USCCR's mission is to inform the development of national civil rights policy and enhance enforcement of federal civil rights laws. They pursue this mission by studying alleged deprivations of voting rights and alleged discrimination based on race, color, religion, sex, age, disability, or national origin, or in the administration of justice. They play a vital role in advancing civil rights through objective and comprehensive investigation, research, and analysis on issues of fundamental concern to the federal government and the public. Their journal *Civil Rights*, along with other relevant publications, is available on their website.

## Urban Institute

500 L'Enfant Plaza SW
Washington, DC 20024
(202) 833-7200
website: www.urban.org

The Urban Institute attempts to provide unbiased, authoritative insights that inform important choices about the well-being of people and places in the United States. As a nonprofit research organization, they believe decisions shaped by facts, rather than ideology. They provide facts that have the power to improve public policy and practice, strengthen communities, and transform people's lives for the better.

Reports on their website include "Gender and Property Rights" and "Housing Discrimination in America: Lessons from the Last Decade of Paired-Testing Research."

# Bibliography of Books

Sharon K. Anderson and Valerie A. Middleton. *Explorations in Diversity: Examining the Complexities of Privilege, Discrimination, and Oppression.* New York, NY: Oxford, 2018.

Gregg Barak, Paul Leighton, and Allison M. Cotton. *Class, Race, Gender, & Crime: The Social Realities of Justice in America.* Lanham, MD, Rowman & Littlefield, 2018.

Jeffrey S. Brooks and George Theoharis. *Whiteucation: Privilege, Power, and Prejudice in School and Society.* London: Routledge, 2018.

Ta-Nehisi Coates. *Between the World and Me.* New York, NY: Random House, 2017.

Marty Gitlin. *Black Lives Matter.* New York, NY, Greenhaven: 2019.

Kelly Glass. *Looking at Privilege and Power.* New York, NY: Enslow, 2019.

Herb Goldberg. *The Hazards of Being Male: Surviving the Myth of Masculine Privilege.* Ojai, CA: Iconoclassics, 2009.

Duchess Harris and Heidi Deal. *Male Privilege.* Minneapolis, MN, Abdo: 2018.

Frances E. Kendall. *Understanding White Privilege: Creating Pathways to Authentic Relationships Across Race.* New York, NY: Routledge, 2013.

Jamila Lyiscott. *Confronting White Privilege Within and Beyond the Classroom: Tools for Inspiration and Action.* London: Routledge, 2019.

Stephanie Y. Mitchem. *Race, Religion, and Politics: Toward Human Rights in the United States.* Lanham, MD, Rowman & Littlefield, 2019.

Paula S. Rothenberg and Soniya Munshi. *White Privilege: Essential Readings on the Other Side of Racism.* New York: Worth, 2016.

Judy Ryde. *White Privilege Unmasked: How to Be Part of the Solution.* London, Jessica Kingsley, 2019.

Brittany C. Slatton and Carla D. Brailey. *Women and Inequality in the 21st Century.* New York, NY: Routledge, 2019

Beverly D. Tatum. *"Why Are All the Black Kids Sitting Together in the Cafeteria?": And Other Conversations About Race.* New York, NY: Basic, 2017

David J. Thomas, *The State of American Policing: Psychology, Behavior, Problems, and Solutions.* Santa Barbara, CA: Praeger, 2019.

Anna Wenzel. *Male Privilege.* New York, NY: Greenhaven Publishing, 2020.

Naomi Zack. *White Privilege and Black Rights: The Injustice of U.S. Police Racial Profiling and Homicide,* Lanham, MD: Rowman & Littlefield, 2015.

# Index